TO DEAN McINNES,

The MBA PROGRAM FOR Physicians AND dentists Changed my life —

Kudos to DR. Jim Hoffman, his crew, AND TTU.

"For Leadership in the micro-organizations of medical practice, Joel has found his voice and is destined to leave a legacy of leadership change."

Chris Fuller
CEO of Influence Leadership and author of *Ididarod Leadership*

"As a serial entrepreneur with extensive healthcare experience, I can say with confidence, Dr. Small has captured the essence of what it takes to bridge the gap between the science of learning and the art of leadership. Any small business owner or success oriented practitioner wanting to create a culture and legacy of excellence would ignore this book at their own peril."

Kevin Weaver,
Author of *Re_Orient*
President and Chief Idea Evangelist, It's Feasible L.L.C.

"Dr. Small has given us a leadership recipe of transformational proportions. He has shown us that value-based leadership is not an accident or a birthright, but a purposeful state of being that is obtainable for everyone who seeks it."

Stephen F. Schwartz, DDS, MS
Past President of the American Association of Endodontists
Chairman, Assurance Biosciences, Inc.

HOW SMALL-BUSINESS OWNERS ARE
CREATING CULTURES OF EXCELLENCE

FACE
TO
FACE

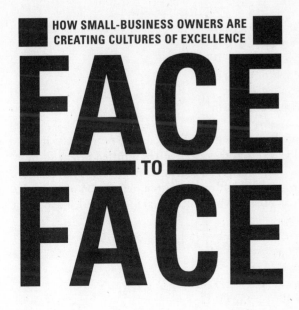

HOW SMALL-BUSINESS OWNERS ARE
CREATING CULTURES OF EXCELLENCE

FACE

TO

FACE

A LEADERSHIP GUIDE FOR HEALTH CARE
PROFESSIONALS AND ENTREPRENEURS

DR. JOEL C. SMALL

HIGHERLIFE
DEVELOPMENT SERVICES, INC
Oviedo, Florida

Face to Face: How Small-Business Owners Are Creating
Cultures of Excellence
by Dr. Joel C. Small

Published by HigherLife Development Services, Inc.
400 Fontana Circle
Building 1 – Suite 105
Oviedo, Florida 32765
(407) 563-4806
www.ahigherlife.com

ISBN 13: 978-1-935245-42-1
ISBN 10: 1-935245-42-1

Cover Design: Principle Creative

First Edition
10 11 12 13 — 9 8 7 6 5 4 3 2 1

Printed in the United States of America

For my mother,

Helen Small.

You are my hero!

Acknowledgments

If you have ever written a book, you probably understand how a cave dweller lived—at least I do. Being the cave dweller is the easy part, however. Living or working with the cave dweller is infinitely more difficult. Like most modern cave-dwelling authors, I owe a great debt of gratitude to all those who supported me and allowed me to take a middle-age sabbatical from my personal life while writing *Face to Face*.

To Brenda, my wife and best friend for thirty-eight years, who would pass by my lair and wave, or bring me food and coffee while I was working, I owe my greatest debt of gratitude. You sacrificed a great deal so that I could realize my dream.

To my children, Jennifer, Zach, and Abby, and to Jennifer's husband, Bennie, I offer thanks for teaching me what it means to be authentic, because they would never accept less from me. My twin grandsons, Caden and Braden, have rekindled my ability to appreciate life with the unbridled joy of a child.

To my brothers, Dr. Neal Small and Dr. Stuart Small, my sisters-in-law, Cherie and Patti, and my extended family of nieces and nephews, I am extremely grateful for the joy that you bring to my life. I am proud of each and every one of you.

It would have been impossible to have written this book without those that were watching the store while I retreated to my cave. Kathy Hamilton, DDS, MBA, my partner in Phase Two Associates, LLC, has been an inspiration and avid supporter of my effort. My partners at North Texas Endodontic Associates, Drs. David Witherspoon and John Regan, two extremely talented clinicians, researchers, and teachers, have been close friends and great mentors.

My staff at NTEA has always been there for me in every way possible. You are an incredible group of people. Together, we have created something quite special, and I feel very fortunate to have all of you in my life.

There is an ancient proverb that says: *When the student is ready, the teacher will appear.* Such has been the case throughout my life. My professional mentors, Dr. Frank Trice and Dr. Steve Schwartz, both being past presidents of the American Association of Endodontists and great leaders in their own right, were the best possible mentors for a young dental student turned endodontist. Although Frank is no longer with us, both he and Steve have had enormous influence in my professional life.

Another influential group of teachers who have impacted my professional life are Dr. Jim Hoffman and the faculty of the Rawl's College of Business. I learned so much from Jim and the faculty at Texas Tech University. The MBA course for physicians and dentists was a wonderful learning experience that gave me a new and exciting view of dentistry and the health-care profession in general. Jim also taught me how to think strategically, a new and useful skill.

To Tammy Kling, my writing mentor and indispensible aid, I owe many thanks. Your insightfulness and skill helped guide me through the challenging process of committing my thoughts to words and bringing my words to life. Thank you. Thank you. Thank you!

Without question, the two most influential people in my life have been my parents. Al Small was as authentic as they come. BG, as he was known to his grandchildren, believed that there was no greater blessing in life than the love of family and friends. He was a man of great integrity and compassion. We miss him dearly.

Helen Small, my mother, is an inspiration to me as well as to everyone who knows her. After raising three sons, sending each of them to medical or dental school, and caring for my dad in his final months, Mom decided to fulfill her lifelong dream of returning to college to complete her undergraduate degree.

At the age of eighty-three, Mom returned to college. Having a wonderful sense of humor, an inquisitive mind, and a lifetime of worthwhile experience to share, Mom became a favorite of students and faculty alike. She graduated with an undergraduate degree from the University of Texas at Dallas at the age of eighty-seven, but she wasn't done yet. At the age of ninety Mom received her Masters degree in Psychology from UT Dallas, and since has taken a position with the Center for Vital Longevity, a University-of-Texas-funded research center for the study of the aging brain, where she lectures on the benefits of lifelong learning. Add to that a book that she will soon publish on the subject of education for senior citizens, and you can begin to appreciate the enormity of her accomplishments.

My mother is oblivious to age. In her late eighties, she traveled to Italy with a group of undergraduates as part of a university-sponsored summer program. That was nothing compared to the following summer, when she spent a week on a marine research vessel off the coast of Texas as part of another university-sponsored course she elected to take.

Mom was telling me that she received a call from the photographers that took her graduation picture at her Masters graduation ceremony. They had lost track of which graduate belonged to what picture and they were trying to decide which graduation photo was my mother's. She told them what she was wearing, the color of her hair and her eyes, and everything else she could think of to describe herself. I couldn't help but ask her the obvious question: "Mom, did you tell them that you're the ninety-year-old?"

"No!" she replied, "I never thought to mention it."

Mom, you have created an example and a legacy for our family and multitudes of people. We could not be prouder of you or love you more.

Foreword

What does it mean to achieve greatness? What does it mean to create an organizational culture that reflects the essence of who you truly are? And how does your organization become a magnet for high performance staff? These are some of the questions that my friend and colleague, Dr. Joel C. Small, has answered in his book, *Face to Face*.

My entire professional career has revolved around helping high achievers obtain a level of operational mastery by focusing on strategy and acceleration. It doesn't matter what industry you're in or what product you offer. If you're operating with excellence, you're going to win.

Joel and I became acquainted years ago when he asked me to help refine his endodontic practice. Like many of my high performance clients, Joel had already achieved a high level of professional mastery. His endodontic practice was, in my opinion, among the top practices in America, but he wanted to do more. That's just the type of person that Joel and other top achievers are.

Joel is one of the more-high-energy people that I know. In a span of four years, Joel returned to school to acquire his MBA, he cofounded Phase Two Associates, LLC, published numerous scientific and practice-management articles, and wrote a book. He accomplished all of this while engaged in full-time endodontic practice. If you ask Joel how he was able to accomplish all of this, he modestly replies that he has a great passion to learn and to teach, and his passion is the source of his energy.

Joel is passionate about leadership. *Face to Face* combines the thoughts and research findings of many of today's top business minds with a dose of real-life homespun insight from Joel's thirty-plus years of clinical practice. He has mastered the unique ability to transform leadership principles from the megaworld of corporate America to the microcosm of a small enterprise. His message is both thoughtful and compelling for those who seek a better way to live and to work.

Joel is a special man with a special message. He's a consummate professional with a passion for sharing his many blessings with his fellow colleagues. I know that you will grow and benefit both personally and professionally from reading Joel's book, *Face to Face*.

Tony Jeary

Author, speaker, executive coach

Author of *Strategic Acceleration, Speaking From the Top,* and *Success Acceleration*

Tony Jeary ™

The RESULTS Guy

www.TONYJEARY.COM

Table of Contents

Introduction

When it comes to leadership, size does matter. Most of the leading books about leadership are from the perspective of corporate America. Most traditional MBA programs utilize case studies of large corporations as a preferred teaching method. And that's okay, if you're the CEO of a large corporation. But entrepreneurs face different challenges. There is little written about leadership and management of small enterprises. When it comes to a microenterprise—a business, like most heath-care practices, which by definition employs ten or fewer employees—there is even less information available. Yet microenterprises represent a significant and growing portion of the U.S. economy.

While conducting my leadership research, I was able to observe leadership as it is applied in corporate America. More importantly, I was also viewing it from the perspective of an entrepreneur and owner of a microenterprise. I was able to recognize that, along with the universal principles of leadership, there are nuances that apply exclusively to smaller enterprises. For example, as organizational size becomes smaller, leadership becomes more personal. Numerous studies have verified my own experience and belief that in a smaller enterprise, the leader's core values have more of a direct impact on the overall culture of the organization. This is clearly the result of the size of the business. A large corporation has a structured leadership hierarchy which creates trickle-down leadership, but a microenterprise is, by its very size and nature, more intimate. Leadership takes place on a face-to-face level in small businesses.

Microenterprises do not utilize mid-level managers or human resource departments to interpret edicts handed down from upper-level leadership. In a microenterprise, the owner/manager is the de facto leader. His or her relationship with members of the organization is likely to be on a first-name basis. Unlike leaders in the more impersonal environment of large corporations, I know everyone in my practice. I know their names. I know the names of their spouses and children. I know what they like and dislike. I know what motivates them. We celebrate anniversaries and birthdays together with cake and songs. Christmas parties are often held at my home.

North Texas Endodontic Associates is a family, and I make it a point to know and understand each and every member of my family to the best of my ability. It is equally significant that they know me. They know what I believe and what I value. They know that I am consistent in my actions. They can predict how I will react in any given situation. They know what makes me happy and what disappoints me. And most importantly they know that I care for them.

"The shadow of the leader" is a phrase, commonly applied to business culture, that speaks to the fact that the leader's beliefs and character are at the heart of organizational culture. Along with this reality comes a degree of accountability. Each and every practice has a culture. That culture can exist by design or by default. Whether good or bad, we as leaders are the creators, teachers, and guardians of our organizational cultures.

So, size does matter. But there is another reason for writing this book. My MBA training made it painfully clear to me that the vast majority of health-care professionals have no basis for understanding the transformational impact that effective leadership can have in our personal and professional lives. Sadly, time does not allow us the luxury of leadership or management training in our crowded medical or dental curriculum. It is my hope that the message of this book will help enlighten our health-care educators to the importance of leadership as an essential and pervasive aspect of quality-oriented health care.

On a more global level, there is an urgent and critical need for leaders to emerge from within the health-care industry. We are desperately in need of leadership that can provide a unifying voice that will direct the future of our professions. We crave a common view to protect us and our patients from those that would diminish the role of the health-care provider by replacing us with bureaucrats. Such leadership can only come from those of us that intimately understand the critical nature of the doctor-patient relationship.

Some of you may be disappointed that this book will not offer a step-by-step formula for becoming a values-based leader. There is a reason for this. Values-based leadership is founded on the authenticity of the leader, and it is impossible to teach someone to be authentic. I am only able to reveal to you my authenticity, and in attempting to replicate that, you will lose the authenticity that makes you unique and effective as a leader.

Understand from the outset that there is no right or wrong when it comes to authenticity. People have a hard time embracing that concept. This fallacy is at the core of many leadership training courses. Creating leaders through a "connect-the-dots" approach is ineffective because the underlying assumption for this approach is that in order to lead we must possess certain predetermined capabilities in order to be the "right" person. In reality we must be a "real" person. No one can teach us to be real.

In spite of this disclaimer, I intend to provide insights and examples that will help guide you in discovering your real self as the starting point in your journey to becoming a values-based leader.

My friend and fellow endodontist, Dr. Kirk Coury, speaks and writes about marketing for specialty dental practices. He tells a story of growing up in a small west Texas town. His uncle owned the Chevy dealership in town, and his dad was the general manager of the dealership.

Every year when the new cars arrived, Kirk's dad and uncle threw a big party at the dealership. The entire town came out for the party celebrating the unveiling of the new cars. Kirk and his brothers were in charge of detailing the cars. They polished the cars until they sparkled. Then Kirk would drive them onto the showroom floor and park them in front of a wall that was covered in floor-to-ceiling mirrors.

The assembled crowd would "oooh" and "aaah" as Kirk drove each car onto the showroom floor. Then each family would inspect the cars. Mom and Dad would sit in the front seat; the kids sat in the back. They would smell the distinctive new-car smell, feel the leather seats, turn all the knobs on the dashboard, honk the horn, listen to the radio, and kick a few tires. Then for a long moment, they would stop everything they were doing and look in the mirror to see themselves behind the wheel of this magnificent car and dream about what it would be like to own it.

My goal is to provide you with this kind of experience when you read about leadership. I want you to feel an emotional connection, and yes, maybe even a spiritual connection to leadership. I want you to have a visceral sense of what it means to lead, and then look into your mental mirror to see yourself personally and professionally transformed by it. I want this image to be so compelling that there is no turning back once you commit to becoming a value-based leader. And finally, I want you to share this knowledge with others.

Chapter 1

Why Lead?

"A funny thing happens when leaders consistently act in alignment with their principles and values: They typically produce consistently high performance almost any way you can measure it—gross sales, profits, talent retention, company reputation, and customer satisfaction."

Fred Kiel—*Moral Intelligence*

L eadership will not just happen by accident. Neither will greatness. If we as practice owners do not purposefully engage in the process of personal and professional development as leaders, we cannot expect the impossible to happen. There is a pervasive reality that I have found to apply to every heath-care practice. Simply stated, the greatest limiting factor in your practice is you. Your practice will only grow and blossom if you grow and blossom. To expect otherwise is to deny reality.

Have you ever experienced a great corporate culture where everyone seems truly happy to be there? The employees have a good attitude, the customers seem at ease, and the energy in the environment is positive and contagious. It's a culture where people are valued, and talents and gifts and personalities are celebrated and recognized. The opposite of this type of culture is the fear-based business. It's an environment in which everyone is afraid to make decisions—and it's disempowering.

When it comes to the question *Why lead?*, the answer is right in front of us. Leaders lead powerful cultures that are personally and professionally fulfilling to all participants. The business thrives because people love being there, enjoy working in it, and share in the rewards of success. Employees take ownership in the decisions and feel connected to customers. It goes beyond good, to great.

Values-based leaders believe in the value of people. They understand that it is much more than money that creates a happy and fulfilling work environment. They know this because it is much more than money that brings them joy and fulfillment as a leader.

Great cultures do not just happen. They are the expression of an evolutionary process through which good leaders become great leaders. This evolution is purposeful and begins with the willingness and determination on the part of the leaders to step out of their existing comfort zones and to challenge themselves in order to grow and achieve a higher level of purpose and meaning in their lives. Only then, after they have struggled and grown personally, can they manifest their greatness within their organizations.

Not every leader is willing to leave their comfort zone. It is often said that good is the enemy of great because the comfort of remaining good is often more compelling than the uncertainty and challenge of becoming great. The lack of compulsion for us to leave our comfort zones is compounded when we lack knowledge with regard to leadership and therefore have no clear vision of what benefit we will derive from the effort.

I have always believed that good practices can be managed, but great practices must be led. The question often asked, however, is: "What's wrong with a good practice?" The argument often goes like this: If I can manage my practice and make a decent living while working four to four and a half days a week, why should I feel compelled to become a leader?

Being from Texas, I have become accustomed to hearing the often-quoted statement, "If it ain't broke, don't fix it!" Implicit in this statement is the assumption that one would know when something is broken. Sadly, this is the exact dilemma that we as health-care practitioners face with regard to leadership. Since we have no leadership training, we have difficulty understanding the transformational power of leadership. Without this basic knowledge we struggle when trying to envision how leadership can transform broken aspects of our practices. Even more importantly, our lack of familiarity with leadership prevents us from understanding the transformational potential of leadership in our personal lives.

So what is in it for us? What are the rewards for making the effort to become a great leader? We have to see some significant value to make the effort worthwhile. The rewards are significant, and choosing to embrace leadership can become a life-altering decision. Let's look at the facts.

LEADERSHIP MAKES GOOD BUSINESS SENSE

It increases productivity and profitability:

There is a danger that if the owner/manager chooses not to lead, he or she may attempt instead to replace leadership with management. This is a particular danger for health-care practitioners who have had little training or exposure to the art and benefits of values-based leadership.

In recent years, several dental management/ consulting firms have promoted a form of "results-based" management. This is the antithesis of values-based leadership. Results are a poor substitute for values, especially when they replace values as the practice "anchor." This reversal of culture in which results drive values has proven to be a poor form of management. No matter what the espoused qualitative values of the leader, in a results-based practice the staff sees the obvious lack of alignment between the stated values and the actual behavior of the leader. It is important to note that our staff sees and learns what we value by observing what we choose to reward and punish as well as how we utilize the practice's resources. When we reward or punish behavior based on predefined performance numbers, we send an incredibly negative message to the staff.

I have observed the destructive nature of results-based management through interaction with several of my referring practices that have adopted this form of management. My assessment of this form of management has been repeatedly corroborated by research that has proven the superiority of "qualitative" versus "quantitative" cultures. There is a profound irony in the fact that numerous research findings unquestionably prove that qualitative, values-based cultures that stress values over financial gain are more productive and have a better bottom line than businesses that adopt a quantitative, results-based culture.

It makes perfect sense, for example, that people commit to values, not to rules or results. (People comply with rules.) Committed people tend to enjoy their jobs and exhibit longevity. Longevity of staff promotes continuity in the practice, and happy staffs are significant determinants of satisfied customers in a service industry. Satisfied customers exhibit brand loyalty, which results in repeat business and drives the bottom line.

As leadership skills increase, management problems decrease:

In her article published in the Journal of the American Dental Association in 2001, Anita Jupp notes, "An overwhelming percentage of dentists report that staff-related issues, not clinical dentistry, are the number one cause of stress in their offices." Does this sound surprising? All of us have heard this common refrain from fellow professionals: "If I only had to worry about treatment issues, and I didn't have to deal with staff, life would be grand!" Those who truly understand the nature of values-based leadership seldom lament their troubles with their staffs, because more often than not, they have valued and supportive staffs that work to make their lives easier.

Forging a supportive staff requires effective communication and role modeling to create a culture of commitment. Conversely, poor communication— arguably the number-one cause of staff problems— frustrates this goal. By clearly communicating our practice culture's values and purpose through both words and actions, we can serve as a catalyst for developing a culture that fosters commitment by all of its members. An axiom of communication is that as clarity increases, ambiguity decreases. Staff uncertainty or ambiguity, as a result of poor communication, creates practice problems and drains our energy by interfering with our ability to maintain focus.

An ideal practice culture would be one in which the leader communicates the culture's core ideology with crystal-like clarity. In this scenario, there is no longer ambiguity or uncertainty. Every team member knows precisely what is expected of him or her and is able to decide with certainty whether specific actions are congruent with the culture's values and purpose. More importantly, when clarity prevails, poor or inappropriate actions become painfully obvious not only to the perpetrator but to the entire team. Cultures that maintain clarity of purpose and values become self-policing cultures. The entire team has decided that chronic, inappropriate behavior will not be tolerated.

Leadership improves staff retention and recruitment:

Over my thirty-plus years in private endodontic practice, I have noticed that the better practices, with effective leaders and well-developed cultures, have much less turnover than other practices. I know of practices that have retained staff for twenty to thirty years. Many of these team members have no financial need to work. They simply enjoy their work because they see value in what they do, and they enjoy being part of a team that is committed to commonly shared values and purpose. Such an environment does not develop spontaneously. At its core you are likely to find a leader that has purposefully created this culture.

Another observation that I have made is that these very same practices have little difficulty attracting excellent people as members of their practice teams. It seems as if these practices become magnets for exceptional talent. Perhaps this is a result of the self-policing nature of a strong culture. In our practice, for example, the staff makes the final decision on new hires. I have complete confidence that my staff has a clear vision of what we collectively expect from our fellow team members. I never worry about them choosing the wrong person because I know that they are extremely protective of our culture. They would never allow someone to jeopardize what we have built together. Interestingly, it is usually the staff that also decides when someone is not aligned with our core ideology and needs to be let go. A culture in which clarity prevails is like a finely tuned and trained marching band. Someone who is out of step sticks out like a sore thumb.

Leadership creates a more fulfilling environment:

There is a striking difference in perception between workers and managers when questioned about the connection between pay- and work-related motivation and fulfillment. Workers will routinely list money as the fourth or fifth most important motivating and fulfilling factor when it comes to their work. Routinely, they will place greater value on interesting, challenging, or meaningful work, along with recognition and appreciation, a sense of accomplishment, and growth opportunities. Each of these valued factors relates to their personal fulfillment.

Managers, on the other hand, when asked about what they perceive to be the motivating factors for workers, will consistently list money as the primary motivating factor. This represents a huge disconnect with significant implications. Managers consistently attempt to motivate workers by throwing money at them, and workers become increasingly dissatisfied because it is fulfillment, not money, that motivates them. The chasm grows increasingly wider as managers begin to feel that the workers are lazy and unappreciative, while the workers see their jobs as unfulfilling and their managers as uncaring.

Values-based leaders recognize the importance of adequate pay, but the significant difference is that they, like their followers, understand that financial gain is most fulfilling and motivating when viewed as a form of recognition for a job well done. By creating a culture that values initiative, creativity, and accomplishment, we are able to motivate others while creating a happier and more fulfilling work environment. Money, as we have seen, is a poor motivator, and rules and regulations are a poor substitute for values and purpose as the cornerstone of an organization's culture. Consequently, a results-based culture fosters compliance rather than commitment and is characterized by low morale and constant turnover.

Even more central to this discussion is the distinction between "transformational" and "transactional" leadership. Transactional leadership style is based on a quid pro quo relationship with the follower. Simply stated, the follower provides a service in exchange for a reward, or in this case, a paycheck. Additionally, a common feature of transactional leadership is the establishment and mandatory compliance with numerous rules and regulations.

Transformation implies change. With regard to leadership it implies a significant and positive change within the followers that is brought about by a transformational leader. Such a leader is able, through leadership skill, to compel his/her followers to align their own individual needs to the needs of the organization. The leader-follower relationship becomes synergistic in that both parties experience higher levels of performance, commitment, and fulfillment based on a mutually shared purpose and mutually shared values.

The difference between transactional and transformational leadership has been the subject of numerous intellectual discussions over the past twenty-five years. The consensus is that people will commit to shared purpose and values. They will only comply with rules and regulations.

Leadership fosters commitment:

How can we ask someone to commit to something when we have not defined what that "something" is? This question may seem to be simplistic in nature. In reality, it happens every day in health-care practices, and in many small businesses. As owners/managers of businesses, we all expect commitment from our staffs, and if asked what that means, we offer a vague comment like, "I expect them to be loyal." Loyal to what? How is such loyalty evaluated? No wonder there is so much uncertainty and ambiguity among our staffs. We create our own worst problems because we are either unaware of the importance of clearly defining and communicating our values and purpose, or because we are unwilling to accept the responsibility of leadership. Remember that leadership is one of very few responsibilities that we as practice owners cannot delegate. And, if we choose to create our ideal environment through effective leadership, we must begin our journey at home. We must first begin with us.

Edgar Schein, one of the world's most noted authorities on organizational culture, states in his landmark book, *Organizational Culture and Leadership*, that there is a critical relationship between the strength of an organization's culture and its leadership, size, communication, and structure. Microenterprises, because of their size and the familiarity between the leaders and followers, are more directly affected by and focused on the owner/manager's personal core ideology. As such, it is the leader's responsibility to create the organization's culture by first defining his/her own personal, deeply held values and core purpose. This, then, becomes the "something" to which we seek our staff's commitment.

LEADERSHIP HAS PERSONAL VALUE

Leadership creates harmony between our personal and professional lives:

Bill George, in his bestselling book *True North*, describes a process that he calls "integration." This is the process through which a person discovers his or her authentic self and masters the art of being that same authentic self in each aspect of life—work, family, friends, and community.

Values-based leaders are the masters of integration. There is no duplicity in their lives. They are effective leaders because of their authenticity, and they are the same authentic person in their private as well as their professional lives. They define their goals based on who they want to be as defined by their values and purpose. For them, achieving a goal in one aspect of their lives enhances and benefits all aspects of their lives.

The concept of authenticity has roots in social psychology. In the mid 1950s, Leon Festinger, a noted American psychologist, presented his theory of cognitive dissonance. This theory suggests that psychological stress is created when there is a difference between our ideal selves and our real selves. The greater the separation between the ideal and the real, the greater the degree of discord or dissonance. Those who exhibit authenticity would theoretically experience no discord because their real and ideal selves would be the same in all aspects of their lives.

The secret to achieving integration is to define with crystal-like clarity who and what we want to be, and to make this vision the anchor for all that we do. This is not as simple as it may sound, but the effort is greatly rewarded. Achieving authenticity brings harmony to our lives by allowing us to be who we have chosen to be in any environment. Along with this harmony comes the greatest reward of all—a profound sense of peace.

Leadership brings clarity to our lives:

Clarity is an important piece of the leadership puzzle. Many of the great minds in the field of leadership consider the ability to provide organizational clarity to be the essential purpose of leadership.

Core ideology is the catalyst for clarity. Core values and purpose, when viewed as our personal and professional foundations, or anchors, are perpetual reference points that serve as a guide and catalyst for effective and efficient decision-making.

If we are authentic values-based leaders, we maintain the same anchor and are benefitted by the same clarity in all aspects of our lives. Foremost among the personal benefits of clarity is our enhanced ability to make difficult decisions. Clarity of purpose allows us to maintain a laserlike focus on what is important. There is a clearly defined path to our goal, and with the resulting absence of uncertainty, we are able to quickly identify and avoid false paths or detours that drain our energy. The end result is that we are able to make effective decisions more efficiently while preserving our energy and avoiding the frustration of distractions.

Leadership defines purpose:

"Leading in today's world requires communication that is substantially different from what was needed only a decade ago. Leaders still communicate the facts, the information that is necessary to make and implement a decision. For this, leaders must be logical, suggesting that moving from where we are to where we are going is a needed, cogent, and doable change. But they also must constantly communicate the 'why' that makes the action meaningful."

Terry Pearce—*Leading Out Loud*

There is no one who understands the significance of purpose better than a true leader. The process of becoming a leader requires a deep understanding and alignment with purpose, and one's purpose in life is the answer to "why" one exists. A true leader derives his or her ability to lead from a strong base forged from a profound understanding and commitment to purpose, and the exercise of developing this base has long been considered a rite of passage to leadership.

Purpose makes a significant difference in our lives because it creates focus and instills motivation. These two ingredients—focus and motivation—are the keys to making things happen. Focus enables us to concentrate on what is important, or essential, to achieving our purpose or goal. Motivation is the mental state that compels us to act or move toward a desired purpose or goal. Ultimately, it is our focus and motivation that enable us to work efficiently and effectively.

Having a common purpose in our personal and professional lives allows us to communicate and instill a sense of this purpose in our followers. This basic principle of leadership is not context specific, nor is it specific to certain types of leadership. Whether we are great military leaders going to battle or organizational leaders going to board meetings, our success is directly related to our ability to communicate a collectively shared purpose to our followers. If you look deep enough, you will find that at the core of every great organization is a leader who has the ability to move people toward a common goal by clearly defining their collective organizational purpose.

There is a wonderful story about the Manhattan Project that I believe illustrates this point quite dramatically. The story is told by Richard Feynman, the eccentric and brilliant Nobel-Prize-winning physicist who, along with Robert Oppenheimer, a brilliant physicist as well, helped coordinate and manage the Manhattan Project. In order to fully appreciate the context and the unique historical perspective of this project, a brief history lesson is required. The time is 1942; the United States is at war with Germany. It has come to the attention of several key people, including Albert Einstein, that the Germans are working feverishly to develop an atomic bomb. Einstein, in 1939, had written to then-president Franklin Roosevelt to inform him of Germany's intention to create a weapon of mass destruction. Subsequent letters from Einstein ensued, informing the president of the urgency of the situation. In 1942 it became apparent that America might be losing the nuclear race with Germany. All agreed that this was a race America could not afford to lose, and in 1942 the Manhattan Project was born. The site chosen for the project was Los Alamos, a small, secluded town in northern New Mexico.

What followed was a massive collaboration between the United States military and our nation's scientific community. The foremost American scientists and engineers of the time were summoned to Los Alamos under a veil of secrecy that many historians would describe as unprecedented. Entire families, uprooted from their homes and extracted from their communities, were relocated to a crude, military-style compound.

Shortly after their arrival, the work at hand was begun. Teams of scientists and engineers were assigned the task of solving equations and creating scientific formulas that would ultimately enable us to unleash the power of the atom. The work was tedious and the days were long. The military, ever vigilant about maintaining the veil of secrecy, would not allow Oppenheimer to inform the teams about the nature and ultimate goal of the project. They were simply given their tasks with no explanation of their significance. According to Feynman, who was in charge of supervising the teams, chaos ensued. The work progressed slowly and the quality of the work was substandard considering the unique qualifications of the assembled talent.

Realizing that something had to be done, Feynman approached his superiors and requested that the recruits be given full disclosure of the project's purpose. Eventually the superiors acquiesced. Robert Oppenheimer gathered the recruits together and delivered a speech that fully addressed the nature of the Manhattan Project and the team's contribution to its success. Following that meeting with Dr.

Oppenheimer, the environment was profoundly altered. Feynman described the change as nothing less than a "total transformation." Oppenheimer had opened the flood gates by simply answering the question *Why?* From that point forward, their efforts had purpose. The culture of the Manhattan Project changed. The quality of work improved exponentially and the deadlines were met with time to spare. Teams became self-motivated, requiring little supervision, and they worked tirelessly around the clock. The rest, as they say, is history.

Finally, it is imperative that we understand our essential role in defining purpose for ourselves and our organization. On one hand, we can motivate individuals by creating a "command and control" culture that demands compliance to rules and regulations and fosters no well-defined sense of purpose. On the other hand, we can create a culture that does not simply motivate, but rather instills motivation, by answering the question *Why?* and clearly defining the organization's collective purpose.

Leadership teaches the art of authentic expression:

If I were to choose the most distinguishing characteristic of values-based leaders, it would have to be, without question, their ability to express themselves authentically. The authentic expression of self is at the heart of leadership because it engenders two of the essential prerequisites of leadership: trust and credibility.

It is my personal belief that authentic communication has a self-evident quality that somehow disarms our natural defense mechanisms and allows us to communicate at a much deeper level of meaning. It is as if we are being approached by someone who has laid down his or her sword and shield and says, "I come in peace." It is their very willingness to be vulnerable that triggers our willingness to respond in kind. Communicating on this level frees us from the concerns of hidden agendas and duplicitous intent which detract from our ability to hear the intended message.

Stephen M. R. Covey, in his excellent book *The Speed of Trust*, writes about the negotiations that led to the merger of their family business with the Franklin Quest Corporation to form the FranklinCovey Company. Stephen, the son of the noted author Stephen R. Covey, represented the family business in the negotiations that eventually led to the merger. At one point the negotiations became quite contentious. The possibility of a future merger looked bleak. Stephen openly admits that he made significant mistakes with regard to his handling of the negotiations. The most critical mistake, according to him, was assuming that his reputation alone would be sufficient to create trust between the two merging entities. This assumption, in fact, was not true. Concerns about trust, hidden agendas, and the overall unfairness of the negotiations were prevalent throughout their numerous meetings.

At the low point in their negotiations, Stephen was scheduled to facilitate a pivotal meeting in Washington, DC, between the key decision-makers for both sides. The purpose of that meeting was to discuss the strategy issues relating to the merger. Realizing that the merger was doomed to failure without a foundation of trust between the parties, Stephen threw out the meeting agenda. He decided to address all of the underlying, unspoken issues that no one had previously been willing to address. The meeting which was scheduled for two hours became an all-day event. Stephen became authentic himself, talking openly about the lack of trust between the two parties. He revealed how it had led to misinterpretation of each party's intentions. By the end of the day, a new sense of trust was created that allowed the negotiations to move forward in a positive, cooperative direction. One leader's act of transparency and vulnerability changed the course of their negotiations and led to the successful culmination of the business merger.

Mastering the art of communicating authentically has significant implications in our personal lives as well. For some, it has helped repair and redefine their relationships with their families and friends. For others, it has improved the overall quality of their lives by enhancing their ability to communicate at a deeper and more meaningful level. At a minimum, authentic communication helps us create harmony between our real and ideal selves.

TAKE-HOME MESSAGES FROM CHAPTER ONE

- Qualitative cultures that stress values over financial gain are more productive and have a better bottom line than businesses that adopt a quantitative, results-based culture.

- People commit to values. They comply with rules and regulations.

- Management problems decrease as leadership skills increase.

- Purpose creates focus and instills motivation in our organizations.

- High-performance organizations with mature cultures become magnets for talented staff and have a high degree of staff retention.

Chapter 2

Finding Ourselves

"As we become more obsessed with succeeding, or at least surviving, in that world, we lose touch with our souls and disappear into our roles. We sense that something is missing in our lives and search the world for it, not understanding that what is missing is us."

Parker Palmer—*A Hidden Wholeness*

S ome readers may ask, "What does finding ourselves have to do with leadership?" The answer, in a word, is "Everything!" Our sense of self defines our deeply held values and our life's purpose— the cornerstones and foundation of our personal and professional life. At its core, leadership is the self-expression of these values and that purpose.

Author and coach Jim Clemmer states the following with regard to self identity: "Reputation is what people think I am. Personality is what I seem to be. Character is what I really am. Our goal should be to blur the lines between the three until they are one and the same." Another well-known educator, theologian, and writer, Parker Palmer, speaks of the need to lead a life of "wholeness," in which we no longer live separated from our true selves. He claims that leading a divided life of multiple identities will eventually diminish our ability to distinguish our true selves from the façade.

These and many other great thinkers have identified the need for self-identity as a key ingredient in achieving fulfillment in our personal lives. Interestingly, this same source of nourishment and enrichment for our personal lives is equally as necessary in our professional lives—especially when it comes to leadership

Many of us struggle to identify our true sense of self. Why? One reason is that for many of us, the development of identity, or sense of self, is not a deliberate, self-directed process. Often we mistakenly confuse our identity with our reputation.

There is a significant difference between our self-identity and our reputation. Our sense of self is derived internally. Reputation is a product of how others define us rather than a product of intentional self-analysis. The problem with defining ourselves as others see us is that we are prone to accept this definition as our true identity simply because this is the path of least resistance. The reality, however, is that self-identity—whether it is based on reputation or character—is a vital reference point for us as human beings. Each of us must decide if we are willing to face the truth about ourselves in order to develop our authentic self-identity. Or, do we take the path of least resistance by allowing our identity to be defined by others?

As a young man, I was a good athlete and played high-school football in Dallas. Upon graduation, I attended a major university on a football scholarship. During my freshman year I suffered a season-ending shoulder injury. In spite of intensive rehabilitation, the same injury reoccurred during my sophomore season. Shortly thereafter my collegiate athletic career ended. It was afterwards that I became aware of a sense of bewilderment and anxiety, which lasted for several years. Lacking emotional maturity, I was unable to identify the cause of my distress. Now, as an adult, I realize that when I quit playing football I lost my identity. Up to this point in my life I had taken the path of least resistance by accepting my reputation as an athlete and adopting this as my authentic self. Once my identity as an athlete was gone, I had nothing to fall back upon. I was so young and emotionally immature at the time that I was unable to realize that being an athlete said nothing about the deeper, more meaningful aspects of who I am—and it was these aspects of my being that would endure as a lifelong reference point for me as a person.

The longer we live what Parker Palmer calls the "divided life," the longer and harder will be the journey back. My own journey back to my authentic self, even at a young age, was difficult. Imagine the emotional trauma experienced when, at midlife, some realize that they have spent a significant portion of their lives being distant from their true selves, and that they have been living in denial of who they are and what they value. Their journeys back would undoubtedly involve the difficult task of rethinking and altering years of thought and behavior that, although based on unrealistic self-identity, has become habitual. The emotional repercussions will often require professional help. As adults, we are more likely to see the advantage of establishing our true identity at a young age. Unfortunately this is not obvious to us when we are young.

Since starting Phase Two Associates, a dental brokerage firm that deals in transitions for dental specialists, I have had the honor of speaking to young specialty residents throughout the country regarding their transition into private clinical practice. I always make a point of visiting with the residents about their future and the importance of finding fulfillment in their personal and professional lives. I begin by acknowledging the fact that most specialty residents graduate with a significant amount of debt. I understand that paying off debt and making a living are foremost on their minds. This has not changed since I entered private endodontic practice over thirty years ago. Having acknowledged these facts, I ask them to do two things. First, I ask them to look into the future to a time when they have paid off their debt and have achieved a level of financial success. I then ask them to consider the journey that brought them to this point in the future. Looking back, do they see a path of happiness embodied by a loving family, friends, and personal fulfillment? Or do they see a path of scorched earth representing regret, failed relationships, and estranged families?

Second, I ask them to consider establishing their goals based on whom they truly want to be rather than what they want to do. By doing this, they are actually adhering to the basic leadership principle of utilizing core values as an anchor for goals. If they follow this suggestion of basing their goals on what they want to be, they will almost always choose the previously mentioned path that leads to a future of happiness and fulfillment.

An article in the Harvard Business Review resonated with me. The primary author, Bill George, has written many books related to leadership, including the best seller *True North*. This paragraph from that article clearly summarizes our quest for leadership and authenticity:

> *When the 75 members of Stanford Graduate School of Business's Advisory Council were asked to recommend the most important capability for leaders to develop, their answer was nearly unanimous: self-awareness. Yet many leaders, especially those early in their careers, are trying so hard to establish themselves in the world that they leave little time for self-exploration. They strive to achieve success in tangible ways that are recognized in the external world—money, fame, power, status, or a rising stock price. Often their drive enables them to be professionally successful for a while, but they are unable to sustain that success. As they age, they may find something is missing in their lives and realize they are holding back from being the person they want to be. Knowing their authentic selves requires the courage and honesty to open up and examine their experiences. As they do so, leaders become more humane and willing to be vulnerable.*

Passion = Energy:

Remember this equation, because in the realm of leadership, this equation is as vital as $E = MC^2$ is to physics.

According to Stephen R. Covey in his book *The 8th Habit*, "Passion is the fire, enthusiasm and courage that an individual feels when he or she is doing something they love while accomplishing worthy ends, something that satisfies their deepest needs."

Great leaders are driven by great passion. One of the distinguishing characteristics that I have noticed when observing great leadership is that the exceptional leader possesses an abundance of energy and enthusiasm for his or her work. I have come to realize that the importance of passion, when viewed in the context of leadership, cannot be overstated. It is passion, derived from our core principles and purpose, and a belief in the collective synergy found within our organization that drives us as leaders and resonates throughout our organizational communities. It is our passion and energy that inspires others to align with our cause. Whether we are leading a large, multinational, billion-dollar corporation, or a small health-care practice, we must maintain and nourish our passion so that we may continue to serve this vital function as organizational leaders.

When visiting with younger dentists, I describe dental practice as a marathon. I find this metaphor appropriate because I often observe a sprinter's mentality in newer practitioners. Those of you that are passionate about running understand the fundamental differences between sprinters and marathoners. The psyche of the sprinter revolves around speed. The marathoner's mentality is geared for endurance. In order to achieve their goals, the sprinter must be explosive, whereas the marathoner is measured. Sprinters mentally train for massive expenditures of energy over a short distance. Their hours of training and preparation are manifested in a matter of seconds. Marathoners, on the other hand, understand they must conserve energy over a long distance. They train mentally and physically for the long haul.

Imagine what would happen if the sprinter attempted to run a marathon. The answer, as you might well imagine, is obvious. He would run out of energy, or burn out. A sprinter is simply not mentally or physically geared to run a marathon.

The same is true for health-care practitioners. A career in health care favors the marathoner. We must adopt a marathoner's psyche in order to successfully compete. And yet, I have seen those who have begun the marathon of health-care practice with a sprinter's mentality. They explode onto the scene, convinced that the speed with which they can acquire material success is the key to winning the race. They begin by leading the pack. But, like the sprinter, their focus is only on the short distance. Reality sets in when they realize that they were focusing on the wrong goal. At this point they are disillusioned as well as being physically and mentally spent; they have burned out.

Each of us has either experienced burnout or known a colleague that has. It afflicts young and old as well as new and seasoned practitioners. The initial physical sign of burnout is an extreme lack of energy. The accompanying mental symptoms are loss of clarity and focus. The etiology is almost always a loss of passion.

Remember: Passion is our source of energy as practitioners and leaders. With the loss of energy and the accompanying loss of clarity and focus, it is difficult to find the motivation and the mental acuity to locate the path back to our core values, purpose, and passion. Separated from this vital source of purpose and direction, we are confused and lost. Just ask some who have been through this potentially life-altering event and were fortunate enough to find the path back to regaining their passion and purpose. They, more than anyone, understand the meaning and importance of regaining and maintaining their passion.

Defining success:

At the heart of our sense of self is an essential question that each of us must answer: "What is our definition of success?" This may be a simple question, but the answer is powerful and will ultimately help define us as human beings. Warren Buffet, the richest man in the world, a man whose name is synonymous with wealth and self-made fortunes, has his own definition of success. In an article entitled, "10 Ways to Get Rich, Warren Buffett's Secrets That Can Work for You," Buffet identifies the ability to determine the meaning of success as a critical factor in achieving "real wealth." You see, despite Buffett's billions, he has never measured success by dollars. In spite of his whole life revolving around amassing an enormous fortune, he's always measured his success in terms of fulfillment. According to Buffet, making large amounts of money is the easy part. We have all seen people do that. The real question is, at what price? At the end of the day when they've created wealth for themselves and others, what kind of life have they created? Has their definition of success been one that stresses fulfillment?

I often remember my early experiences attending the American Association of Endodontists meetings. In the mid 1970s we were a small group and a relatively new specialty in dentistry. Our original founding fathers, who had written all of the textbooks, were in attendance at the meetings. I remember feeling awestruck in the presence of many of those great people. Fortunately, my mentors at the dental branch in Houston were also very involved with the AAE. They were always thoughtful enough to introduce me around and include me in their dinner plans at the meetings. As a result of their generosity, I was able meet many of these brilliant people. Over the years I became friends with many of them.

I will never forget a conversation I had with one of my friends who happened to be a past president of our organization. It was at one of our national meetings, and we were attending a reception hosted by one of the meeting sponsors. I told my friend how I had admired him for his contributions to the field of endodontics, and how much I valued his friendship. He thanked me for my sincere expression of admiration and friendship, and then he began to tell me how he and others like him had admired me for the person I had become.

I was astonished by what I was hearing. He said that they admired the fact that I was still married to my wife Brenda after what was then twenty years (it is now thirty-eight), and that I was a committed father to my three children. They admired me for seeking fulfillment as the source of my success.

I already knew that my friend had paid a heavy price for his fame and position. He was past middle age, divorced from his wife, and estranged from his children. Beneath his words I heard his remorse for choices he had made earlier in life.

Of course my life has also included a quest for financial success, like anyone else. You don't become an entrepreneur without lofty business and financial goals. But from that day forward I knew that having money without someone to share it with, or to have money and fame at the expense of fulfillment, was an empty existence. That moment made me a better person and a more effective leader.

Finding our voice:

Finding our voice is an expression of synergy in which the harmonization of our individual skills, knowledge, experience, and sense of self creates a seemingly effortless and subconscious expression of ourselves that far exceeds the sum of our individual talents.

Some refer to being "in the zone." Others have used the expression "finding your stride" or being "in the groove." All of these expressions refer to a physical and psychological harmony that, once achieved, creates an elevated state of acuity in which goals are achieved in a seemingly subconscious and effortless manner.

Think back to your first childhood experience of riding a bike. I'm sure that most of us will agree that the learning phase was the hardest part. It resulted in a few falls, possibly some bumps and bruises. But once we got the hang of it, riding a bike became second nature. We never again had to consciously think about the mechanics of riding a bike. Even years later, not having ridden in a long time, we can still hop on a bike and take off riding.

Leadership is a lot like riding a bike. The learning phase requires a serious examination of our deepest selves. This may be a challenging and painful experience. There are often emotional bumps and bruises along the way. But once we get the hang of it, leadership is like riding a bike. It becomes second nature.

Artists, writers, and musicians often speak of a similar experience. They refer to finding their voice. For them, this represents the confluence of study, training, experience, and personal expression that culminates in their own unique style. It represents one of those pivotal moments when their capabilities no longer operate independently, but spontaneously align to create a harmonious expression of their creativity and talent.

The same experience is possible for us as individuals and leaders. Like most aspects of effective leadership, personal discovery precedes professional development. Finding our voice is no different.

People often fear leadership because of the iconic and larger-than-life qualities that our culture has attributed to our leaders. Many view leadership with the reverence reserved for leaders like John Kennedy, Martin Luther King, or Ronald Reagan. Without question, these were truly some of the most iconic leaders of our time, and few people could imagine themselves being a leader of this magnitude. In reality, however, some of the greatest leaders of our time were people that never saw themselves as great leaders. They were able to find their voice by placing their message and their cause ahead of themselves. They are the ones who have learned that leading from behind is often more effective than leading the charge from out in front. Their predominant qualities include character over charisma, an unwavering resolve to succeed over expediency, and self-expression over self-promotion.

Darwin Smith, the CEO of Kimberly-Clark from 1971 to 1991, was such a leader. He is credited by many industry analysts as being a brilliant leader that was responsible for refocusing and rebuilding the company into the largest paper products company in the world. In spite of his exceptional leadership skill, Darwin Smith was anything but the prototypical iconic leader. He was a shy man who rejected notoriety and publicity. His coworkers were not likely to describe him as charismatic. Yet he masterminded and led one of the most significant resurrections of any company in the twentieth century. Many would say that his success was based on his resolve to succeed. For him, failure was not an option.

For leaders who have found their voice, leading appears to become second nature. Almost effortless. These are the special ones who appear to have it all together. There is no hesitation or second-guessing their decisions. Leading for them becomes an intuitive experience. These are the ones that we admire the most and seek as our mentors.

TAKE-HOME MESSAGES FROM CHAPTER TWO

- Our sense of self is the foundation of leadership.

- Sense of self is derived internally and defines our character. Our reputation is derived externally and represents what others think of us. Value-based leadership relies more on character than reputation.

- Self-identity is a vital reference for us as human beings and leaders.

- Create goals based on who you want to be rather than what you want to do.

- Great leaders are driven by great passion. Passion = energy.

- We must broaden our definition of success to include fulfillment.

- Great leaders find their voice, place the message above themselves, and understand how to lead from behind.

Chapter 3

The Qualities of Leadership

"In our research we tried diligently to discover the one, two, or three capabilities that were common for all extraordinary leaders. We failed. Our research confirms what has been suggested from clinical studies of organizations and leaders. There clearly is no one pattern that covers all organizations, nor leaders within any one organization. Our data support the conclusion that effective leadership is incredibly complex and diverse. Providing one simple key to leadership is just not workable. Our inability to find these universal issues was in many ways one of our most profound findings."

John Zenger—*The Extraordinary Leader*

As I stated previously, leadership cannot be taught by a "connect-the-dots" approach. The difficulty of teaching leadership becomes most apparent when we realize that we cannot agree on a definition of what it is that we are attempting to teach. If you read the work of people like Jim Collins, Ken Blanchard, John Maxwell, or many of the great business scholars that write today, you will find hundreds of descriptions of a leader. Capabilities required for effective leadership are both industry and organization specific. For example, an industry that is undergoing dynamic change will require different capabilities from its leadership than a stable industry. Similarly, organizations within the same industry will likely have their own specific leadership requirements based on the context or current environment of the specific organization.

In spite of the widespread disagreement among scholars with regard to leadership, certain universally accepted qualities are attributed to effective leaders. Since I am most qualified to speak from the perspective of a small business owner, I have included some of the qualities of leadership that I believe apply to the world of a microenterprise.

A leader is acutely self-aware:

"Values–based leaders are self-aware, instilling their personal values to shape corporate culture:

*a values-based culture that drives extraordinary
results. Values-based leaders understand that
what they believe and value determines how they
behave, that how they behave impacts the model for
organizational behavior (culture), and that specific
behaviors generate predictable and sustainable
corporate performance.*"

Davis H. Taylor

I have a colleague who struggles with his identity as a dentist. He is continually changing his practice philosophy. Initially he wanted a high-volume, well-advertised, restorative practice. He built a large office that was beautifully decorated. He advertised extensively, and he offered lavish bonuses in the form of trips and spa days for his staff if certain production goals were met. This practice was productive for a short time, but eventually declined.

Then he decided to travel a different path, adopting the "lean and mean" philosophy. He fired a majority of his staff, moved to a smaller office, and became very frugal when it came to expenditures. In a short period of time, the remaining staff left. The practice has since become a revolving door for disgruntled employees. The lack of continuity in the staff has caused the practice to lose patients and production.

This same colleague continually attends practice-management courses. To his staff's dismay, he returns from each seminar ready to take the practice in a new and different direction. Not having attended these seminars, the staff is understandably unable to share the doctor's enthusiasm. They have become frustrated by the lack of consistency in the practice, and this has led to the high staff turnover.

My colleague is constantly looking for the answer to solving his practice's woes—never realizing that he is, in fact, the problem. He has no sense of himself either personally or professionally. He has no anchor that prevents him from being blown along with the prevailing wind.

Values-based leaders believe that their core ideology serves as their highest priority. They have paid the price to identify their deeply held values. They are seldom blown off course, because they are guided and anchored by these principles.

Leaders are fully engaged:

I recently was attending a dental conference in Dallas when I ran across the staff of one of my colleagues. They were attending a program that I was hosting. The topic was on leadership, and the speaker was exceptionally knowledgeable and a wonderful presenter. I noticed that the doctor was not with the staff members. At our first break, I inquired about his whereabouts. They said that he was attending another "more technical" session that happened to conflict with our session. I simply nodded and thanked them for coming, but I was thinking to myself about what a terrible message he was sending to his staff. I felt certain that the doctor had no idea of the degree to which his lack of engagement was undermining the culture and development of his practice. What's even more unfortunate is that this is not an isolated incident.

Being engaged means that we commit ourselves willingly and fully to our cause, and by doing so, we inspire others to engage as well. Engagement is an unspoken act that speaks volumes about who we are. It is also one of the most meaningful ways of letting others observe what we truly value. With regard to leadership, the difference between engagement and disengagement is critically significant.

Engagement = Commitment

Disengagement = Compliance

Disengagement is a hallmark of default leadership. The resulting culture is one of compliance, because it is impossible to create commitment when we choose to lead through emotional absenteeism.

Personal engagement means deploying all of our personal resources—time, energy, skill, and knowledge—to serve our cause. Only fully engaged leaders can successfully create a culture of commitment for their practice, because others will not commit unless the leader shows them the way. It's like soliciting a charitable donation for a worthy cause. Friends and colleagues are unlikely to make their donation unless they know that you have made yours first.

Leaders are exceptional communicators:

"To effectively communicate, we must realize that we are all different in the way we perceive the world and use this understanding as a guide to our communication with others."

Anthony Robbins

Our sense of self means little if we are unable to bring it to life within our practices. As aspiring leaders, bringing who we are to what we do is an essential prerequisite for values-based leadership. We each have within us our message of purpose and value that must be shared with others. Our ability to clearly communicate this message, both verbally and nonverbally, distinguishes us as leaders.

Because of the nature and size of our practices, we have a much greater opportunity to inspire and motivate others than do leaders in the larger, more structured organizations. Studies on the dynamics of leadership in small organizations indicate that our influence as owner/managers—along with our ability to communicate on a face-to-face basis with our staff— affords us tremendous power in determining and affecting the standards and performance of our practices. It is the clarity of our message that will ultimately determine the degree to which it is adopted within our practice culture. As we develop this concept, it will become apparent that we are solely responsible for the message that is heard.

Several years ago I worked with Brian DesRoches, PhD, a clinical psychologist from Seattle. He has extensive experience as a coach and mentor working with dentists in developing leadership skills. Brian's strengths are in communication and personal development. It was my work with Brian that taught me to be 100 percent responsible for my communication with others. His guidance helped me realize that what I mean to say is irrelevant. What is heard is what is truly relevant. More importantly, it is my responsibility to insure that the message delivered and the one received are the same.

In my thirty-plus years of practice, I have emphasized this point to members of our practice team. Patients do not always hear what we have told them. In an endodontic practice this is particularly true because many of our patients come to us anxious and in pain, both of which have a way of altering a patient's ability to hear and process information correctly. Often the message that the patient hears has no similarity to the message that was intended. When misunderstandings occur, I visit with my office staff to better understand what transpired. Invariably, the misunderstanding is the result of miscommunication on the part of our office. The problem has to be ours, because by accepting responsibility for both the message delivered and the message received, we become the guilty party by default when miscommunication occurs. It may be a bitter pill to swallow, but when it comes to communication, perception is reality, and when a misunderstanding arises as a result of poor communication, it is almost always because the person delivering the message has not taken responsibility for what was heard.

Leaders are role models:

"What you do speaks so loudly that I cannot hear what you say."

Ralph Waldo Emerson

There are two essential parts to communication: the verbal and the nonverbal. Many of us would agree that the nonverbal form of communication is the most powerful. We may be exceptional orators. Or we may be lousy. But at the end of the day, if our actions do not match our words, it doesn't matter. Everything that we verbally communicate—every value, every purpose or principle that we have tried to instill in our practice culture—can be undone with a simple contradictory action. It is a costly mistake to assume that incongruence between our stated values and our actions will go unnoticed. Our office staff, our families, and our friends are aware of actions that give a false impression of our values.

If there is one pearl that you will take away from this book, I hope that it will be the realization that your unspoken message is every bit as powerful as the words that you speak. Nothing could be truer with regard to leadership and the culture that is derived from it.

When coaching young practitioners, I urge them to establish their core ideology first, and to use their purpose and values as the guiding tenets for everything that they do.

We all agree that being financially successful is a universal goal of every for-profit enterprise. But the paradox exists. Organizations that stress values and quality-of-life issues as an integral and foundational basis of their culture will ultimately be the more financially successful enterprises. My message to these young dentists is that they can indeed have it all. Being an authentic values-based leader who esteems purpose and values will ultimately deliver sustainable financial reward. Stressing productivity over values and purpose will not yield the same result.

Merck Pharmaceuticals, a company known for its social consciousness, was faced with a defining moment in the company's history in the mid 1980s. At that time there was a disease known as river blindness that swept through the African continent. The disease was carried by a black fly that bred in the rivers of Africa. The fly, through its bite, would inject a parasite beneath the skin where it would multiply and grow. Eventually, the parasite would gain access to the blood system and travel to the eyes, causing complete blindness. At this time there was no known remedy.

Merck happened to be working on a vaccine for a totally separate bovine parasitic disease and through serendipity discovered that this vaccine also produced immunity to river blindness. Merck applied for funding to help distribute the vaccine to the affected countries. Unfortunately, neither the countries, the United Nations, nor any other humanitarian organizations had the funds or the mechanism to distribute and administer the vaccine.

Merck's stated core purpose was "to preserve and improve human life." Their values statement went on to say that "all of our actions must be measured by our success in achieving this goal." Merck was faced with a significant dilemma. How could they act consistently with their stated core purpose and respond to the obvious dire needs of so many Africans and still maintain their corporate and fiduciary responsibilities to their stakeholders?

Fortunately, Merck's leadership at the time was values-based. They understood the nature of the dilemma, and based on their core ideology, they pursued what they felt was the obvious solution to the problem. Merck, at their own expense, manufactured large quantities of the vaccine. They also set up and funded the mechanism through which the vaccine would be distributed and administered throughout Africa. The final expense absorbed by Merck was an astounding 100 million dollars.

Other worldwide health organizations, inspired by these magnanimous actions, have since partnered with Merck in establishing an ongoing program to provide the vaccine, free of charge, to underdeveloped countries throughout the world that are affected by river blindness.

Many industry leaders were initially skeptical of Merck's decision to donate their vaccine and establish a perpetual program to insure its availability. In spite of the initial skepticism, this program has since been hailed as the benchmark of corporate social responsibility. Today, similar industrywide programs have been developed. Other companies have looked at the Merck experience and how it has enhanced their corporate values and corporate image in ways that Merck had not originally anticipated.

A different story tells a contrasting tale of the consequences of actions that contradict stated values.

Jim Clemmer tells an insightful story about a large corporation that hired him to conduct a full-day seminar for their entire management team. The corporation had initiated a new internal campaign that stressed the importance of balance in the lives of their employees. The campaign had been introduced the previous year at the yearly management conference, the topic of which was family values.

Jim arrived early for this year's seminar and was enjoying breakfast while visiting with some of the management team members. He inquired about the previous year's meeting, and realized immediately from their reaction that this topic was an open wound. Apparently, last year's meeting began on a Monday, and each of the attendees was required to arrive at the meeting location on Sunday night. This required considerable travel time for each of the attendees. Unfortunately, the Sunday before the meeting was Father's Day. You might well imagine how this experience affected the corporation's image and their organizational values in the eyes of their managers who had to travel on Father's Day so that they could attend a corporate-sponsored seminar on the importance of family values.

Situations similar to this, in which thoughtless action overshadows seemingly thoughtful words, are a common occurrence. This scenario creates what I refer to as the "rhetoric-reality gap," in which there is a direct contradiction between words (rhetoric) and actions (reality). Invariably, the actions, rather than the words, provide meaning to the experience.

We often create a rhetoric-reality gap unknowingly and in spite of our good intentions. I personally came to this realization when my staff informed me that by micromanaging I was expressing a lack of trust in them. I was astounded by this revelation, because I truly trust my staff. I know that they are extremely capable. One of our shared values is trust, and yet I was sending a nonverbal message that directly contradicted it. After this experience, I began to look for other ways that my actions contradicted my stated values and beliefs. This, by the way, is an exercise that I would recommend to all of those that assume a leadership position. You likely will be surprised, as I was, at how often our actions unknowingly contradict our words.

Values-based leaders enhance their preferred culture by continually working to reduce the gap between rhetoric and reality. They understand that words alone cannot create the trust that is so vital to building and maintaining their practice culture. They understand that winning the hearts and minds of their followers is not a matter of saying things right;

rather, it is a matter of consistently saying and doing the right thing.

Leaders believe in abundance:

"People with a scarcity mentality tend to see everything in terms of win-lose. There is only so much; and if someone else has it, that means there will be less for me. The more principle-centered we become, the more we develop an abundance mentality, the more we are genuinely happy for the successes, well-being, achievements, recognition, and good fortune of other people. We believe their success adds to...rather than detracts from...our lives."

Stephen R. Covey

I love the idea of abundance. I don't see abundance as a philosophy. I see it as a lifestyle. People who lead an abundant lifestyle see their universe as infinite. They demand win-win scenarios in their personal and professional lives. In their world it is not just acceptable for everyone to succeed. It is an imperative.

Compare this to a lifestyle of scarcity, or what some call a zero sum philosophy, in which the universe is viewed as finite. This particular outlook requires that for every winner there must be a loser.

I often compare the two lifestyles to pizzas. One is a cosmic pizza that is a never-ending supply of food for all that want to partake. A cosmic pizza is never depleted. The other is a medium pepperoni pizza, and for every piece someone eats, there is one piece less for me.

A scarcity or zero sum philosophy is not compatible with effective leadership, because effective leaders are those that are committed to assuring that everyone they lead is given the opportunity and resources to succeed. To an effective leader, realizing one's dreams is a universal goal.

Taken a step further, leaders who embrace a scarcity philosophy believe that their role as leaders is to identify weaknesses in others and judge others on the basis of their weaknesses rather than their strengths. This is a lose-lose scenario, because dwelling on weaknesses seldom creates a positive result for either party.

Abundance-based leaders are the antithesis of scarcity-based leaders. They understand that each of us has weaknesses, but they choose to judge others based on their strengths. Their practices are always more successful because they know how to identify strengths and position their people so that they are able to successfully develop and utilize their strengths. The result is a culture that benefits the practice while providing the employees a sense of accomplishment and empowerment. Also, it has been my observation, and interesting to note, that in the abundant culture which stresses development of strengths, the weaknesses are likely to spontaneously disappear. It is my belief that this is the direct result of a culture that is accepting of failure and views de-emphasizing weakness as a means of developing strength.

An abundance leader who identifies and utilizes others' strengths creates a very different kind of culture than does a scarcity leader who continually tries to correct weaknesses in others. The scarcity-based culture is an overall negative environment. The staff is always afraid to make their own decisions or try new ideas, because failure in itself will be viewed as a weakness and will be dwelled upon. In an abundant culture, the staff is comfortable making creative suggestions and trying out new concepts because they know that failure will be viewed as a necessary part of the growth and development of their strengths.

The contrast between the two lifestyles becomes most obvious when applied to a business model or, in our case, a health-care practice. Imagine a practice culture in which the doctor/leader attributes achievements to their staff and is the first to accept the blame for failures. What would it be like to work in an organization in which the leader was fully committed and engaged in assuring that everyone reached their full potential and realized their individual dreams? This is an organization that will prosper.

Now compare this to a practice culture based on scarcity, in which recognition is coveted by the doctor and seldom shared with the staff. Compare it to a culture in which the leader has an emotional need for control. This scenario—quite different from the abundant culture—will lack spontaneity, creativity, and member development. This is an organization that is in trouble. It will likely crumble because the burdens created by the leader's scarcity mentality cannot be supported by the weakened cultural infrastructure.

Abundant cultures are participative as well as being creative and adaptive. They are able to tap into their vital stream of human potential which is a prerequisite for a highly productive and culturally mature organization. They promote self-development and self-direction. Such organizations are the icons of their industries.

We'll talk more in later chapters about the traits of a negative leader and why managing and leading with fear doesn't equate to a positive bottom line. The point is, we all have a decision to make. Business and life can be joyful and abundant, or they can be stressful and scarce.

Herb Kelleher, the untraditional CEO of Southwest Airlines, said this about his organization's culture: "A financial analyst once asked me if I was afraid of losing control of our organization. I told him I've never had control and I never wanted it. If you create an environment where the people truly participate, you don't need control. They know what needs to be done, and they do it. And the more that people will devote themselves to your cause on a voluntary basis, a willing basis, the fewer hierarchs and control mechanisms you need."

Is it any wonder that numerous studies have proven that organizations that create cultures based in abundance are significantly more profitable than those organizations whose culture is scarcity-based?

Leaders focus organizational energy:

When I speak to groups, I like to wear my hedgehog T-shirt because it offers a nice visual of what Jim Collins refers to in his book *Good to Great* as the "Hedgehog Concept." The hedgehog is very similar to a porcupine. It is a small animal covered in a coat of spikes that serve as protection from predators.

The underlying meaning of the hedgehog concept comes from an ancient parable about a hedgehog and a fox. The parable tells of the hedgehog, which possesses few of the physical or mental attributes of the fox. The hedgehog, although lacking these attributes, does know one thing very well—how to survive.

Each day, when the hedgehog forages for food, the fox, which is smarter but less focused than the hedgehog, makes a new plan for attacking and eating the hedgehog. At some point in the hedgehog's daily forage, the fox emerges from his hiding place to attack the hedgehog, but like the day before, the hedgehog curls up into a spiked ball and thwarts the attack. Baffled by his inability to vanquish the lowly hedgehog, the fox returns to his lair to make new plans for another attempt the following day.

The moral of the story is that, although other attributes are of value, it is the ability to narrow our focus to that which is essential that allows us to survive. The same lesson has significant application to business. History tells of many successful businesses that sought to expand their market share or sphere of influence through ill-conceived mergers and acquisitions, only to lose their focus on what was essential to their survival. The consequences of these actions have proven to be disastrous for most of these companies.

Collins suggests a practical method for narrowing our focus. The answers to three questions, when considered collectively, show us the path. First, what are you deeply passionate about? Second, what can you excel at? And third, what drives your economic engine?

Collins visually represents these questions as three concentric circles. The area of confluence at the center of his diagram represents a similar answer to all three questions, and what will likely prove to be a powerful critical success factor and an area of intense focus for our practices.*

Let me give you an example of how the concept has worked for my own practice. Some years ago, my two partners, Dr. David Witherspoon and Dr. John Regan, and I were trying to decide how we might best market and brand our endodontic practice. After much discussion, a sudden epiphany presented us with a clear and obvious answer to our question. Without knowing, we had answered Collins's three essential questions with a single answer.

Each of us has a passion for teaching. Dr. Witherspoon is a previous recipient of the Edward M. Osetek Educator Award, given yearly by the American Association of Endodontists to the best young endodontic educator in the world. Dr. Regan is an accomplished teacher as well, and I also have previous teaching experience. Both of my partners are recognized researchers and have published numerous scientific articles in various journals and textbooks, both nationally and internationally.

* Jim Collins, *Good to Great* (New York: HarperCollins, 2001), *203*.

There was no question in my mind that we could excel at teaching and research. We already had a proven track record in both of these areas.

Whether teaching and research could serve as an economic driver for our practice was the hardest question to answer; however, it just felt so right. The depth of our passion for education and the degree of our commitment to teach and give back to our dental community was so overwhelming that we would do it for free, and indeed we do.

Each year we donate our time and resources in order to provide a series of free continuing education programs to the north Texas dental community. Additionally, we conduct clinical research in our private practice and publish our research in the form of scientific articles in various national and regional specialty and general dental journals.

To a great extent we have been successful in branding ourselves as competent educators, clinicians, and researchers. The degree to which our brand has served as an economic driver for our practice is hard to quantify, but we have been able to grow and maintain a successful fee-for-service endodontic practice in a period of significant nationwide recession while fulfilling our desire to utilize our unique abilities and pursue our passion.

An observation that I made while conducting my leadership research is that almost every great researcher or author in the field of leadership in some manner addresses the importance of combining capabilities and passion as a key organizational success factor. Some authors may have used different terminology or a different approach, but if we reduce their messages to the essential elements, we will find that passion and skill are often the common denominators for organizational success.

Leaders who narrow the focus of their business will realize that they have also sharpened the clarity of their business's vision. Combine this with the guidance provided by a core ideology, and the business's course and path are set like a laser-guided missile. Knowing where you are going, why you are going there, and the path you will travel is a degree of clarity seldom experienced in any business, and it is this degree of clarity that allows us to make instinctive mid-course corrections when external factors temporarily alter our course. We also conserve precious energy and facilitate our decision-making ability by defining the most direct path to our goal.

Leaders are willing to be vulnerable:

"The deeper our faith, the more doubt we must endure; the deeper our hope, the more prone we are to despair; the deeper our love, the more pain its loss will bring: these are a few of the paradoxes we must

hold as human beings. If we refuse to hold them in hopes of living without doubt, despair, and pain, we also find ourselves living without faith, hope, and love."

Parker Palmer—*A Hidden Wholeness*

As Parker Palmer states, it is through our vulnerability to doubt, despair, and pain that we are able to fully experience the joys of faith, hope, and love. Imagine how shallow life would be if we were unwilling to accept the risk inherent in our vulnerability.

I would venture to say that most people define vulnerability as weakness. If we consider the term in the context of warfare or even business, vulnerability would imply that we have somehow failed to protect ourselves from harm. Whether harm comes in the form of a hostile business takeover or an enemy attacking an unprotected flank, the final analysis is that we, as business or military leaders, have failed. If we look for synonyms for the word *vulnerable* in a thesaurus, we find that they include the words *weak, defenseless,* and *helpless.*

Contrary to this standard interpretation, vulnerability can also be a source of great strength if we are willing to see it differently. Recall the vivid image of an unidentified, unarmed, Chinese student standing alone while blocking the path of a

Chinese military tank in Tiananmen Square during the Chinese worker and student uprising in 1989. This was a display of ultimate defenselessness and helplessness, but the message was one of incredible strength for people around the world. Other great people like Martin Luther King and Mahatma Gandhi have changed the course of nations by the strength derived from their willingness to be vulnerable.

Vulnerability is seldom discussed in relationship to leadership. Yet, a leader who refuses to be vulnerable will never fully achieve the strength and depth of his or her leadership potential. There is no doubt that vulnerability, as displayed by the student in Tiananmen Square, involves risk. At times it involves great risk. As a business leader, being vulnerable may even put your professional career at risk. Some of us may be unwilling to suffer the harm that risk can bring. Others understand that the rewards derived from our vulnerability far exceed the potential risk. For exceptional leaders, it is their commitment to their core values and purpose that enables them to seek these rewards while enduring the risk.

Leaders are willing to trust:

Trust is ubiquitous with regard to leadership. It is strong and pervasive, and yet it is subtle to the point of being almost indistinguishable. It is only one of the many threads woven into the multitextured fabric of leadership, and yet it creates a disproportionate degree of strength and support. Trust is both the precursor and by-product of leadership, and yet through all of this, trust remains unaltered.

Consider the issue of trust as it relates to leadership. Books on leadership mention trust as one of the critical factors in the leader-follower relationship. Most authorities would agree that without trust, leadership is at best ineffective, if not nonexistent. But trust involves a considerable degree of vulnerability on the part of a leader and follower. Trusting others can be potentially harmful, particularly if it proves to be unwarranted.

Those of us that have been emotionally harmed by a breach of our trust feel violated. Our natural tendency is to disappear within our emotional selves and never to trust again. With time, as we recover from our deep cynicism, we ask the key question: "Will I ever again know whom to trust?" The answer is a disappointing *Probably not!* This may be a bitter pill to swallow, but if we are to develop a culture of trust, we, as leaders, must willingly trust others so that they may, in return, trust us. This is one of the paradoxes that, as Parker Palmer states, we, as human beings, (and leaders) must resolve. There are other, similar examples of the strength of vulnerability. Choosing to no longer micromanage others is a great leap of faith that requires vulnerability on the part of the leader. Intuitively, we may understand the negative effect that micromanaging has on staff motivation and creativity. Letting go is still a frightening experience because we have, in our own minds at least, placed the success of our organization in the hands of someone other than ourselves.

It is interesting to note that in cultures characterized by a command-and-control mentality there is a continuous downward spiral in staff morale and productivity. At the core of these cultures is a deep-seated lack of trust on the part of the leadership. Values are replaced with stringent rules and regulations. The team members, perceiving the scarcity of trust and lacking the guidance of values, are often immobilized by their inability to determine the right thing to do. Ironically, this inability to act results in loss of productivity, which the leadership views as a lack of adherence to the rules, and, consequently, more rules and regulations are created. Punishment for further disobedience becomes more severe.

How do we resolve this obvious contradiction, or cognitive dissonance, between our perceived need to trust and our fear of trust? The solution lies in our belief that never to trust again would be to deny ourselves the many meaningful experiences that trusting others can provide. In the final analysis, we are willing to trust in spite of the potential harm because we value the positive aspect of trust more than we fear the potential negative.

When trust is present within a business atmosphere, the employees are empowered to make decisions that will benefit the entire team. Trust can be felt. And it's an element that has the power to transform almost any individual and business. Try adding trust as a core value to your business today. Watch how things change. Say "I trust you" often to your employees and loved ones through your actions and words. Build your business around trust.

Leaders are authentic:

It is hard, if not impossible, to exhibit different forms of authenticity in one's personal and professional lives. Authenticity is by definition "the genuineness or truth of something" and, therefore, with regard to people, must be universally applied to all aspects of life. Stress or dissonance is created when people, lacking authenticity, try to apply a different set of values to their business and personal lives. There is a constant struggle between the two life entities. When these two entities become more congruent, there is a profound sense of oneness and harmony.

Authenticity is highly valued in many cultures. Think, if you will, of some of the most influential mentors in your own life. Now describe their most significant qualities. Look closely at the words you have chosen. Likely you will find the word authentic or its synonym in your choice of words.

We value authenticity for its simplicity. When it comes to authenticity, what you see is what you get. There are no hidden messages, agendas, or complexities.. Authenticity puts us at ease and helps us feel safe in its presence.

TAKE-HOME MESSAGES FROM CHAPTER THREE

- Leadership capabilities are both industry and organization specific.

- Core ideology (purpose and values) serves as our anchor. It prevents us from being blown off course.

- Only fully engaged leaders can create cultures of commitment. They lead by example.

- Effective leadership requires exceptional communication skill and being 100 percent accountable for the message delivered and received.

- We must bridge the rhetoric–reality gap to harmonize our verbal and nonverbal communications.

- "Abundance" leaders believe in helping others achieve their goals. The culture they create is participative, creative, high performance.

- Narrowing our organization's focus helps us concentrate and conserve our organization's energy and resources.

- Vulnerability is a strength in the context of leadership.

- Giving trust is an essential prerequisite to receiving trust.

- At the core of command-and-control cultures is a deep-seated lack of trust on the part of the leadership.

- Authentic leaders share the same core ideology in their personal and professional lives.

Chapter 4

The Culture

"Transformational leadership matters, because it is about changing people and organizations for the better, not just about getting higher levels of productivity. The aim is not to motivate, but to instill self-motivation. Transformational leaders build organizational cultures that not only drive high performance—they sustain high performance. And they sustain people as well. Leaders do this by giving people the opportunity and the capability to make meaning for themselves."

Marshall & Molly Sashkin—*Leadership That Matters*

Culture defined:

There are currently over 160 definitions of organizational culture. Edgar Schein, the author and MIT professor, is commonly credited with inventing the term corporate culture. Schein defines the term as "The pattern of basic assumptions that a group has invented, discovered or developed in learning to cope with the problems of external adaptation and internal integration and have worked well enough to be considered valid, and therefore to be taught to new members as the correct way to perceive, think and feel in relation to those problems."

I'm a simple person, so let me give you a simple definition of culture that works for me. It's the sum total of all the expectations that the organization's members have for themselves and for every other member of the organization. Culture exists within every organization, and it exists whether we recognize it or not. Unfortunately health-care practitioners often pay a heavy price for not recognizing the existence and significance of our practices' cultures. Understanding that practice cultures exist, that they are powerful and transformational, and that we must create them by design will provide the genesis for an infinitely better practice.

The fastest and easiest way to determine the strength of a practice culture is to determine the degree to which the staff shares common expectations of themselves as individuals and as a group. In a practice with a strong culture, all team members will know with certainty what is expected of them and how they should act. The expectations of the team and the doctor will be so deeply embedded in the minds of team members that their actions will be intuitive.

According to Jim Clemmer, today's leaders must recognize that culture is the vehicle that allows them to move their organizations and people beyond success to significance, and in doing so they elevate their entire team to a higher level of development that taps into ever deeper levels of the human spirit and individual needs. Today's high-performance organizations are successful not because they offer tangible benefits in the form of perks or higher wages. Instead, their success is based on their ability to provide for the intangible, deeper-level needs and to provide for their people a sense of connection to something greater than themselves.

The strength of a culture is determined by the degree to which it can clearly define its fundamental guiding principles and beliefs. The clearer these tenets become, the more a potential stakeholder can determine the degree to which they are either strongly repelled by or attracted to the culture. Simply stated, strong cultures clearly define core ideologies that will invoke strong emotional connections between the cultural ideology and those stakeholders that are attracted to it, whereas cultures with poorly defined guiding principles are unable to invoke a similar response because the strength of the emotional connection is diminished by ambiguity and uncertainty.

Ian Percy, in his book *Going Deep: Exploring Spirituality in Life and Leadership*, suggests that corporate organizations are awakening to the reality that most of their problems are spiritual in nature. Organizations that deny this reality do so at their peril because the days of command-and-control organizational cultures are drawing to an end.

Purpose, people, and profit:

We learned earlier that an abundant culture creates a more profitable business. There is an interesting paradox in that the harder we try to create abundance as a means to profitability, the more surely we will fail. Abundance is not a system to be monitored, but rather a philosophy and lifestyle that engenders the leader's genuine commitment to helping those he or she serves to become the people that they need and wish to be.

Tony Dungy, the highly regarded former head coach of the Indianapolis Colts, in his book *The Mentor Leader*, talks about intentional leadership and creating an abundant culture through mentoring:

"As their title suggests, mentor leaders seek to have a direct, intentional, and positive impact on those they lead. At its core, mentoring is about building character into the lives of others, modeling and teaching attitudes and behaviors, and creating a constructive legacy to be passed along to future generations of leaders. I don't think it's possible to be an accidental mentor."

A culture based on a lifestyle of abundance is keenly focused on maximizing the potential of every member. This is one of the powerful magnetic attractions that an abundant culture has for potential participants. People seek employment with businesses that are willing to invest in helping them realize their full potential. Companies like Nordstrom and General Electric and even the United States armed forces are known for their commitment to maximizing their organization's human potential. This reputation becomes an internal brand that attracts a group of people who want to improve their skills and marketability, and in general are self-motivated and possess a strong work ethic.

Exceptional leaders in today's business environment are the ones who are capable of recognizing the potential of their people. Sometimes this potential is obvious, but often it is not. There are tests that can be administered to aid a leader in assessing skills, but the best leaders are those that possess an intuitive ability to see hidden talent. Often our best leaders or managers are hidden in plain sight.

As an example, I would like to share with you the story of Debbie, our office manager at North Texas Endodontic Associates. Debbie has been a member of the NTEA staff for twenty-two years. She has all of the attributes that a practice owner could possibly want from a valued employee. She is bright, self-motivated, extremely loyal, trustworthy, and patient-focused.

Several years ago we had an office manager who left our practice to relocate. When considering her replacement, the doctors agreed that Debbie had the capability to become an excellent office manager, but she lacked some of the managerial skills required for this role. We offered Debbie the job based on her commitment to acquire the necessary skills and our commitment to provide her with the support and resources necessary for her to be successful as our office manager. We hired Jill Tappe, an excellent professional coach, to help Debbie make the transition from receptionist to office manager.

That was about six years ago, and Debbie has since become an exceptional manager and leader not only in our practice, but in our immediate dental community. She is held in high regard by all of our referring doctors and their staff. I often tell her that she is the NTEA icon. She laughs as if I were teasing her, but she knows how serious I am. Helping Debbie to become our office manager was a win-win for both of us. Our practice has greatly benefitted from Debbie's leadership, and providing her with the necessary support and resources has enabled her to become the person and leader that I believe she was meant to be.

Debbie is a prime example of how organizations might address the relationship between purpose, profit, and people. Those organizations that are able to clearly define their purpose are better equipped to develop their people and have been shown to be highly profitable. Conversely, organizations that seek profit at the expense of purpose and people have been shown to be unsustainable.

Jim Clemmer, in his book *The Leader's Digest*, discusses the significance of these relationships:

> *Of course, if a company isn't profitable and financially strong, it won't exist long enough to serve any other purpose. That's the paradox to be managed: Companies that exist only to produce a profit don't last long, while companies that don't pay attention to profits can't exist to fulfill their long-term purpose. I call this the Profit Paradox. The key is to find the right middle ground, because pursuing profits without a higher purpose, or pursuing a purpose without profit, are equally fatal strategies.*

The secret to solving the profit paradox is to prioritize and address each of these issues in the proper order. For example, purpose (priority 1) is what attracts the right people (priority 2) to our organization. Equipping our people with the knowledge, skill, and resources to be successful (priority 3) in order to make our organization profitable (priority 4) is the final part of the solution.

Mission statements:

At this point in a book about leadership, culture, and growing your business, I'd expect to see a chapter on how to start with the end in mind by creating your mission statement and goals. You've seen that before—the fancy mission statement in cursive framed and hung in the most conspicuous spot on the reception area wall. As you can probably tell, I'm not in favor of mission statements for small businesses, although they may be appropriate for some larger corporations. I can understand the purpose, and I've created them in my own life and business. But leadership isn't really that simple. It's not about posting a mission statement on the wall. The purpose of doing that might be to let our employees know our intentions and the goals of the culture we're trying to create, but ultimately great leadership and successful cultures are going to be driven by commonly shared purpose and values. Because of the face-to-face nature of our leadership, our purpose and values will become so pervasive that they will become the mantra of our culture.

Perhaps the epitome of hypocrisy is the leader that disregards the very core ideology that he or she developed but pulls out the mission statement and uses it as a weapon to discipline staff that has acted inconsistently with these principles and values. Unfortunately, this scenario plays out more often than we would like to admit. It is an indication of a failing culture. We cannot make our practices something that we are not. We cannot create a culture of trust or commitment to values and purpose if we, ourselves, are not trustworthy or respectful of our own core ideology.

The profit-based culture:

As business owners we have the unique opportunity of creating a culture by design. Unfortunately, this is often not the primary focus of many new practitioners. Faced with a large education-based debt, the new practitioner is often more concerned about optimizing production in order to create enough income to support his or her lifestyle and service the debt. The practice culture in this scenario will become a by-product of a financially based paradigm, and often will be nothing like a values-based culture. The problem with a profit-based culture is that, once we start down this path, it's hard to reverse course without completely changing the culture of the practice — a difficult task at best.

Through my work with Phase Two Associates, I have encountered practices that have developed a culture based on financial reward. Recently, I was consulting with a very profitable specialty practice that could not seem to keep associates even though the practice was very financially successful. They asked for our assistance in recruiting and maintaining associates that would ultimately become partners in their practice. It was their assumption that they were not recruiting the right people, or that there needed to be a better explanation as to the financial value and reward for ultimately entering into partnership in their practice. They were pleased with many of their previous associates, but over time, the associates would seem to lose their drive and ultimately leave to establish a practice elsewhere.

I listened intently as they explained their benefits, their production, and their compensation formula. It didn't take long, however, for me to identify the problem. A light went off when they explained that their current triggering mechanism for partnership was based on the associate's production. In other words, when the associate was able to produce as much income as the existing partners, she or he was extended an invitation to become a full partner. Often this would take a young associate from five to seven years to accomplish. While this format made perfect sense to the current partners, it seemed very lacking, if not counterproductive, to me. I explained to the practice owners that partnership is the crown jewel in the eyes of a young associate. She or he has worked a long time and endured many hardships to acquire ownership in a successful practice.

More importantly, not every associate wants to join a practice that values them based on their ability to produce income. The world has changed, and many of the new practitioners value flexibility and quality of life issues more than profit.

No matter what their intended message, in the eyes of the associates, their price of admission to the crown jewel of ownership was based on production, and therefore the practice owners must value production more than people. In my opinion, this was the reason that they were unable to keep these young associates in their practice.

I completed my consultation with a suggestion and a warning. I suggested that they take one of two paths. Either (1) they really do value production over everything else, in which case they should look for seasoned practitioners that express a similar practice philosophy and are able to produce at a high level, or (2) they do value quality of life issues, in which case they should change the criteria for partnership to reflect their real values. You see, no matter what they said, the things that they chose to reward or punish sent a message about who they are and what they value that was more powerful than the words they spoke. As I said, I did leave them with a warning. It was apparent to me that these practitioners were highly motivated, hard-driving, type A personalities. I expressed my concern that if they kept looking for clones of themselves that they might ultimately regret receiving what they were asking for. I saw potential problems for their practice culture if they did not include some diverse personalities in their partnership mix. I left this final comment with them as food for thought.

In case you are wondering, we ultimately restructured the buy-in mechanism so that young and promising practitioners would be judged on their overall contribution to the practice, and they were allowed to buy into partial ownership based on their percentage of production after a two-year associateship. This allowed them to become partial owners much sooner. We felt that this mechanism would result in a happier and more committed associate.

Changing a culture:

Hopefully you are beginning to understand what a well-developed culture looks like. It has been my intention to offer compelling reasons for purposefully developing a culture based on commitment rather than compliance. I can imagine that some of you have been nodding your head in agreement because you have done just that. Others of you may be feeling a little uneasy at this point. Perhaps you are realizing that your practice's culture is not the way it should be or could be. Likely you will ask yourself whether you have missed the boat. Is it too late to transform a culture of compliance into one of commitment? And most importantly, how do I go about facilitating this transformation?

I face this issue when advising young specialists as they prepare to take the reins of their newly acquired practices. Often, the culture created by the previous doctor/owner is not aligned with the core ideology of the new practitioner. Decisions made by the new doctor at this critical juncture will have a profound and lasting impact on the foreseeable future of the practice.

Attempting to change a practice culture with no well-developed strategy is like jumping blindly off a cliff and hoping that there is deep water down below. Cultural change is one of the most challenging endeavors that most of us will ever face. It is a slow, delicate, and deliberate process that, as Jim Collins has shown, requires exceptional leadership.

Unfortunately, most new practitioners lack the leadership skill and maturity to effectively change a practice culture. More often than not, their well intended but poorly executed attempt to change their practice culture results in a total cultural collapse. The sequence of events that follow include a loss of most, if not all of the staff and patients, a significant loss of income, and utter bewilderment for the practice owner who has just taken out a large loan so that she or he can own a practice with no staff, patients, or income.

A study of a General Motors plant in Freemont, California, provides one of my favorite lessons with regard to the process and power of cultural change. Although there are enormous differences between an auto manufacturing plant and a health-care practice, the underlying messages are universal.

In the 1950s, General Motors built several production plants in the western United States as part of their "sunbelt strategy." The reason for choosing these locations for their plants was related to the fact that the southern and western states were mostly right-to-work states and therefore were less influenced by the labor unions that were powerful forces in the upper Midwest. The strategy proved unsuccessful, however, and the Freemont plant, along with the other Sunbelt plants, was ultimately organized by the United Auto Workers. The relationship between the UAW and management was at best contentious, and eventually degenerated to a level of downright hostility.

Over time, the hostile atmosphere permeated the entire plant, and the Freemont facility ultimately became the worst producing, most conflict-ridden plant in the GM organization. In spite of numerous attempts by the management to improve morale and boost the production numbers, by the early 80s the Freemont facility had the highest cost overruns and the lowest quality rating of any GM plant. By 1982, the problems were so great that the GM executives designated the plant as being unsustainable, and they closed the Freemont facility.

The facility remained closed for three years. During this time GM decided to attempt a unique experiment at the Freemont facility. They formed a partnership with Toyota, a Japanese auto manufacturer. Toyota was known for its ability to produce an excellent product at a reasonable price. They had fine-tuned the assembly process to an art form that was extremely efficient. Toyota was interested in gaining access to the American market and was therefore enthusiastic about the joint venture. The ground rules for the joint experiment were as follows: GM would provide the Freemont Facility. There would be no remodeling of the facility, and no new equipment would be purchased. GM insisted that due to the existing labor contract, the previous workers had to be offered the new jobs first. These were the same workers that were responsible for the poor performance that led to the initial closing of the plant. Toyota agreed to all of these stipulations with one request, and that was that the facility had to be run by the Toyota management, not GM management. GM agreed, and shortly thereafter the Freemont facility was reopened under new management.

What followed was a complete reversal of the negative trends that had proved fatal for the previous management. In the first year alone, workers' formal complaints went from a previous total of five thousand to a total of two. Only half of the workers were rehired and yet the facility was able to produce 20 percent more cars. Sales trends were positive, profits were increased, and the product quality and customer satisfaction were the highest of any GM facility. The Freemont facility became the J.D. Powers award-winning flagship facility in GM's organization.

The dramatic turnaround of the Freemont plant was directly related to a philosophical change that altered the culture of the facility. Whereas the previous management saw the unions as adversaries and the workers as unreliable, the new management expressed an interest in making the unions and workers partners in a successful venture. With regard to the union, the Toyota management adopted an attitude of cooperation based on mutual respect and trust. As a result of their approach, the Toyota management and the local union signed a collective bargaining agreement in which both parties committed to solving problems together and finding mutually beneficial ways to improve the work environment and increase safety and productivity.

With regard to the workers, Toyota management instituted training programs for all employees. The potential line workers were required to undergo a three-day assessment, which included evaluation of production capabilities as well as group discussions and written tests. Once hired, each worker attended a four-day orientation that included information on Toyota's philosophy, teamwork, safety, policies, and the competitive nature of the auto industry. About four hundred middle management people were sent to Japan for an intense three-week classroom and on-the-job training program at Toyota's Takaoka plant. On a more subtle level, the new management made an effort to break down barriers between the workers and management by doing away with the executive parking lot and executive cafeteria. They also moved their managers' offices to the assembly floor so that management would be more accessible to the workers. Each worker was given a business card with their name and job title in order for them to feel that they were an integral part of the Toyota team.

What I find most interesting is that Toyota was able to bring about a profound and lasting change in the Freemont facility not by cracking a whip, but rather by extending a hand. They were able to break down barriers by developing trust rather than implementing more rules. In his book *The Speed of Trust*, Stephen M.R. Covey makes an excellent point with regard to the destructiveness of distrust in business organizations. He points out that the fundamental belief by leadership that people cannot be trusted becomes a self-fulfilling prophecy, because where there is a foundation of distrust, there is structural hierarchy and excessive rules and regulations, and a strict management mentality predominates. Each of these systems and structures are cumbersome and counterproductive to the development of trust. The result is that the organization is handicapped by leadership that unwittingly creates the very structure that validates their original belief that people cannot be trusted. A vicious and downward cycle ensues, that, in the case of the Freemont plant, led to a collapse of organizational culture.

Covey goes on to state that trust changes everything, and indeed this may be true when it comes to organizational culture. Behind the success of any culture is an underlying trust that all parties will honor their commitment to the core ideology of the organization, and that each organizational member will be held accountable for acting harmoniously with the mutually shared values. This trust is further solidified and imbedded in the culture when the leadership displays consistency in rewarding or punishing behavior based on adherence to these principles. High-trust organizations are also among the most financially successful businesses. According to a study conducted by Watson Wyatt, high-trust organizations outperformed low-trust organizations in total return to shareholders by 286 percent.

When it comes to changing a health-care practice's culture, there is a good news–bad news scenario. The good news is that it can be done. The bad news is that it is not an easy or quick process. I believe deeply that even the most skilled leader cannot change people, at least not when it comes to their essential values and purpose. This power is reserved for a higher authority. We do, however, have the ability to facilitate change in others through the process of influence. Leaders influence followers and transform cultures by serving as an example of what it means to act in harmony with our values and purpose. Our verbal and nonverbal modeling of consistency between actions and beliefs serves as an example for others and transforms our culture. Changing the existing culture of a health-care practice involves creating trust and influencing others to change perceptions and actions that have become habitual, which requires time, effort, and patience. I have observed the negative effect of impatience on the part of some of my colleagues who attempted to force cultural change by implementing change before establishing trust. As we have seen, the net result is a swift departure of a significant portion of the staff.

Unfortunately, some of the departed staff are excellent people. They would have been exceptional team players. They would have likely remained had the doctors realized that in the context of culture, trust must always precede change.

Another interesting reality is that some people are simply adverse to change, even if the change is positive in nature. These are also people who require a structured environment and therefore are initially opposed to any change that will disrupt their usual routine. Even changing from a results-based culture to a values-based culture, something that would be easily accepted by most, may be difficult for those that are adverse to change. These people need time to process the meaning of the intended change. They must internally visualize the nature of the change and understand the benefit to them of adopting it. This may be a slow process. Any attempt by a leader to hurry or expedite the process could be met with rejection. Having said this, once this person accepts the change, she or he will become its strongest advocate and will resist any attempt to alter the newly adopted changes.

While working to create trust as the foundation of a new culture, it is important to simultaneously begin the process of replacing restrictive rules and regulations with values as the guiding principles of the culture. This is not to say that a values-based culture is without rules and regulations. Every organization must have certain rules, regulations, and policies. However, a quote by Émile Durkheim says it all: "When cultural values are sufficient, laws are unnecessary. When cultural values are insufficient, laws are unenforceable."

Most authorities would agree that command-and-control cultures that demand strict adherence to rules and policies are eventually unsustainable. Every great culture is sustained over time by its values, not by its rules or regulations.

Unfortunately, casualties often accompany change. Some of the team members may not embrace the changes that you have endorsed. It is important, however, not to make snap judgments about a given person's willingness to change. Some people have a bad way of displaying otherwise good intentions. For example, team members may possess the values that you desire, but they may also be currently incapable of seeing how their actions are out of sync with their values. Our responsibility is to coach these team members so that they can reach their full potential. This is done by making the persons aware of the problem, and consistently modeling the appropriate behavior. Over time it will become apparent whether the persons are capable of change.

Losing staff as a result of cultural transformation is an unfortunate, but often necessary, occurrence. As Jim Collins points out in the book *Good to Great*, it is the leader's responsibility to insure that the right people are "on the bus." Otherwise there cannot be optimal commitment to the organization's values and purpose. It is also reasonable to assume that someone that does not embrace the practice culture would feel uncomfortable in this environment. Given this scenario, a staff member leaving your practice to find one that is a better match is a winning scenario for both parties and should be viewed as such.

The wonderful thing about adopting a values-based culture is that over time it brings out the best in its members by creating congruence and harmony between what we believe and how we act. According to the previously mentioned theory of cognitive dissonance, it is emotionally painful for most people to simultaneously hold two or more opinions that are logically or psychologically inconsistent. Emotional problems arise when there are significant differences between what we believe to be our ideal selves and what we know to be our real selves. For example, acting inconsistently (real self) with our true values and beliefs (ideal self) will create dissonance or psychological discord that may manifest itself as a feeling of anxiety, tension, or even depression.

Resolving the emotional pain brought on by cognitive dissonance requires that we recognize the existence of our internal and external discord, and purposefully choose to heal our emotional pain by aligning our actions with our values and beliefs. Sadly, those of us that have not identified our authentic self are often unable to recognize the discord and will suffer through the emotional pain for extended periods.

I remember vividly a conversation that I had with an emotionally distraught young lady. She had the misfortune of having worked as a dental assistant for an unethical dentist, who eventually lost his dental license as a result of chronic negligence and substandard care for his patients. I met the young lady as a patient of mine several years after this dentist had sold his practice and moved away. At one point in our conversation I asked how she felt while working for this dentist. She told me that she and all of her coworkers were aware that the dentist was providing substandard care for their patients. She went on to say that the atmosphere in the office was like a cancer that eventually drained the entire staff of their energy and that several of the staff eventually left the practice. But the most interesting thing that she shared with me was the painful aftermath that she had experienced as a result of having endured this cognitive dissonance. You see, she knew that she was part of the neglect and substandard care that was provided for those patients. She knew it, she tolerated it, and she failed to listen to her conscience, which told her to flee this environment.

She unwisely stayed on as a dental assistant for the dentist that eventually bought the practice. This is when the real pain began. She recalled how a former patient, having been made aware of the numerous problems created by the previous dentist, looked at her with tears in her eyes and said, "How could you have let him do this to me?" At this point in our conversation she began to sob. The reality of what she had done was more than she could bear. She not only had to quit her job as a dental assistant, she had to undergo months of psychiatric therapy. She still carries the guilt related to this experience. She could not return to dentistry, and she now works in another industry.

Although this may be an extreme example of acute emotional trauma resulting from cognitive dissonance, the fact is that chronic, low-grade distress is common in cultures that have a behavior pattern that contradicts basic principles of human decency and trust.

Culture versus technology:

Not long ago, I had the opportunity to visit with a young endodontist who had recently purchased an existing endodontic practice. He was seeking advice regarding upgrades for his newly acquired practice. He had a limited budget for new expenditures, and wanted to know if I thought that his limited resources would best be spent for digital radiography or for a cone beam scanner. I responded by asking him what he wanted to achieve by purchasing the technology.

He replied that he wanted to improve the quality of care that he and his staff could offer their patients.

I feel certain that he was surprised by my reply. I told him that spending the money on developing his culture and his people should be his first goal. I suggested a retreat with his staff and hiring a professional consultant and coach with expertise in leadership and team development as a facilitator for the retreat. He admitted that he was unable to see the value in my suggestion because he and the previous owner of the practice shared a similar practice philosophy, and he anticipated very little change as a result of the transition. I assured him that, even though their philosophies may seem similar, his leadership qualities and his expectations of the staff were different from those of the previous owner. I also assured him that quality of care begins with his practice culture.

I feel strongly that investing time and money in a practice's people and culture at a critical juncture of practice transition is the right place to allocate resources. It has been my experience that we too often lose sight of the importance of our staff with regard to their critical role in our practice's success. We frequently make the mistake of believing that technology is more important than people as a key success factor for our practices.

While technology can contribute to growth or greatness if used as an adjunct to a well-developed culture and the correct business strategy, Jim Collins contends that technology by itself is never a primary cause of either greatness or decline. He refers to technology as "an accelerator."

With regard to a health-care practice, technology will accelerate practice growth only if the practice's fundamental core business and cultural principles are in place and functioning. Relying on technology to serve as a primary practice builder is a costly mistake. I have seen this time and time again. One practice may grow exponentially after investing in new technology, while the practice next door languishes in spite of having purchased the same technology. In one scenario, the practice is able to pay for the new technology through increased practice revenue, while in the other scenario the practice does not grow and is saddled with the additional expense of the new technology. The difference between these two practices is that in the less successful practice the doctor sees technology as a quick fix and never examines the underlying issues that are negatively impacting the practice's ability to provide quality service for its patients. The other, more successful, doctor understands that technology cannot create growth, but rather can only enhance the growth of a well-run practice.

In a broader context, technology represents a competitive advantage for a well-run practice. By definition, a competitive advantage is the ability to provide a service or product in such a way that it allows you to maintain a market advantage over your competition. Technology can do this for our practices. The question is whether this advantage is sustainable. Take my practice, for example. We recently purchased a cone beam scanner. We were one of the first endodontic offices in our area to have this piece of equipment. Financial gain was not the only factor in our decision to purchase the scanner. We decided to purchase this technology based on its ability to significantly improve our diagnostic capabilities. We fully understood the temporary nature of any competitive advantage that we might enjoy from being the first to own this technology. Indeed, our competitive advantage was short-lived and disappeared as other endodontists also purchased scanners for their offices.

So what would constitute a "sustainable" competitive advantage? A sustainable competitive advantage is an advantage that is enduring due to its uniqueness or because it is very difficult to copy or reproduce. Warren Buffett often refers to a sustainable competitive advantage as a moat or barrier to entry for another business. This analogy implies that there is a degree of permanent insulation obtained by creating a unique advantage.

In today's environment a sustainable competitive advantage is based not so much on what you provide but rather on how you provide it. Considering this, it is important to recognize that your staff is the primary determinant of how your practice's care is delivered, and as such, your staff and the unique culture that guides them are your most significant sustainable competitive advantages.

No one can duplicate the uniqueness of your culture. Your culture defines your practice as surely as your DNA defines you, and it is because of your culture that patients seek your care and refer their friends and family to your practice. Unfortunately, people often believe that some new technology or "gizmo" can reverse their lagging production. Today's new gizmo is tomorrow's old gizmo, but your practice culture endures and is sustainable.

I'm not suggesting that we disregard technology. After thirty-plus years of endodontic practice, I have witnessed the incredible impact that technological advances have had on the quality of care that we can offer our patients. I am a huge fan of technology, and my office is equipped with all the latest and greatest endodontic equipment. However, we must begin to regard technology realistically. Having the newest technology is the price of admission for an endodontic practice. It is a baseline requirement and therefore does not separate us from our competition.

From my perspective, I have yet to find any form of technology that can possibly affect the long-term success of my practice more than the people who treat my patients every day.

TAKE-HOME MESSAGES FROM CHAPTER FOUR

- Culture is the sum total of all the expectations that the organization's members have for themselves and for every other member of the organization.

- High-performance organizations are distinguished by their ability to meet the intangible, higher-level needs of their people.

- Financially successful organizations have learned to prioritize and address the issues of purpose, people, and profit.

- Changing to a values-based culture requires that the leader first create trust while simultaneously implementing values in place of rules and regulations.

- Emotional discord arises when there are significant differences between what we believe to be our ideal selves and what we know to be our real selves.

- Your culture is the source of your practice's sustainable competitive advantage.

Chapter 5

The Leadership Paradox

"It's much easier to think of examples of firms or individuals suffering from too much management and not enough leadership than it is to think of examples of the opposite problem. There are two reasons for this. First, business schools and universities have done a very thorough job of teaching management skills. They're easily identifiable, easily quantifiable, and easily communicated. Granted, it takes real application and discipline to become a superlative manager, but the skill set involved seems much more readily accessible to most of us. Leadership, on the other hand, is fantastically difficult to get right. Whereas most experts would agree on the essential elements of good management, a much smaller number agree on the tenets of great leadership. And if the skill set isn't even clearly agreed upon, it's not surprising that leadership skills are more often found to be lacking."

Michael Feiner—*The Feiner Points of Leadership*

> *"Most ailing organizations have developed*
> *a functional blindness to their own defects. They*
> *are not suffering because they cannot resolve their*
> *problems but because they cannot see their problems."*
>
> John Gardner

A ccording to a report by Training Magazine, leadership development expenditures by U.S. businesses, as of 2007, has become a twelve-billion-dollar-a-year industry. Leadership development, at 21 percent of total training expenditures, now represents the largest single category of training expenditures by American businesses. This data supports what many industry insiders have come to recognize—American businesses are hungry for leadership training.

In a corporate setting, future executives are trained as managers or as leaders. As they rise through the ranks there are literally thousands of dollars spent in order to provide them with training. Additionally, they are often mentored by experts in their respective fields. Before they assume the positions of top-level executives they are thoroughly prepared for the job.

Most health-care professionals have never had formal training as managers or leaders. Their college and postgraduate curriculums are filled with courses designed to prepare them for the technical aspects of their respective fields.

As health-care practioners, if we fail as leaders it is largely due to a lack of competency rather than character. Over my thirty years in private clinical practice, I have come to appreciate the integrity of the vast majority of my peers. If we have failed in our roles as practice leaders, it is because we never acquired the necessary knowledge to lead effectively.

Jim Collins presents a provocative and thoughtful position on the importance of leadership to businesses in his book *Good to Great*. The book is based on an extensive five-year research study of almost 1,500 Fortune 500 companies conducted by Jim and his research team. Published in 2001, *GTG*—as it has come be called—sold 1.5 million copies in its first three years following publication. It is considered by many to be among the most influential books ever written in the field of business.

Collins and his research team identified eleven companies from their pool of 1,500 candidates that, based on their findings, transformed from good to great. Each of these companies had been in existence for many years and traditionally remained near their industry's average with regard to their yearly stock returns. Each of the eleven target companies underwent a sudden transformation that resulted in a meteoric rise in their stock returns that far exceeded the industry average and was sustained for a minimum of fifteen consecutive years. The team of researchers dissected these target companies to identify certain common characteristics that led them from good to great. The most consistent and compelling finding was that each of the transformed companies had an exceptional leader at its helm at, or near, the time of transformation. No other factor appeared to be as critical to the transformation process as leadership. Are we surprised? Business organizations have long recognized the importance of leadership to their company's success. Leaders are revered in many cultures, and the ability to lead is considered by many to be a god-given talent reserved for a very special few.

Marcus Buckingham, the author of *First, Break All the Rules*, makes the point that leadership and management are inherently different. He presents a summary of a twenty-five year study conducted by the Gallup organization in which they interviewed eighty thousand managers of four hundred successful publicly held companies. The purpose of the study was to define best practices in management. According to Buckingham the mindset and competencies required by managers and leaders are uniquely different.

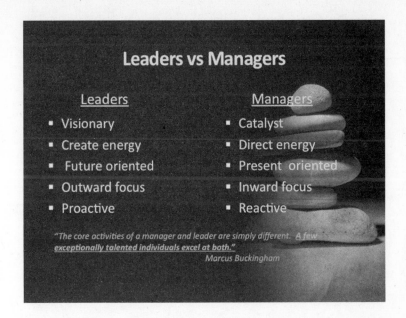

He issues a warning to businesses against assuming that managers are leaders-in-waiting. Buckingham believes managers that are appointed to leadership positions will often fail because a good manager is not necessarily a good leader. Buckingham goes on to say, "The core activities of a manager and a leader are simply different. A few exceptionally talented individuals excel at both." This statement, unfortunately, does not bode well for health-care practitioners who, more often than not, have no training in leadership or management, and therefore no opportunity to develop a talent in either discipline.

At the level of a microenterprise, the difference between management and leadership is much less distinct. As an owner/manager of a microenterprise, a health-care practitioner, with little or no understanding of management or leadership, must serve in both capacities. This creates a worrisome paradox because, according to Collins, our success is based largely on skills that we, unfortunately, do not possess, while Buckingham states that only very few highly trained people possess the competency to both lead and manage their businesses.

New health-care practitioners each face the daunting task of establishing a business that they must somehow manage and lead if it is to be successful. Is it surprising that they often experience a sense of bewilderment? Frustration develops because we are, by nature, problem solvers, and our new business presents many problems and unique challenges that we are not trained to solve. What can we do alleviate this frustration? We can't emulate a large corporation, because the leadership and management structural hierarchy of the larger business does not exist in our small practices. We can adopt some of the basic and fundamental principles of a larger business by scaling them down and adapting them to fit our smaller business model. But as we have seen, as the size of the organization shrinks down to a microenterprise, the rules of the game change.

With nowhere else to turn for help, most of us at some point seek help from colleagues. But the unfortunate reality is that health-care practices are short of qualified mentors because few of us have experience in leadership. Practice management consultants can be of some help, but most consultants are teaching management and calling it leadership.

At some point, however, either from colleagues or consultants, we learn and eventually adopt what I believe has become the traditional form of health-care practice management. It's a form of management that I call systems management. It requires that we set up systems to monitor each aspect of our practice. There is a system to monitor accounts receivable, another system may monitor new patient visits, a third may monitor referrals to specialists, and so on.

The problem with systems management is more in its application than in its design. Systems management is quite simple and can be effective when utilized judiciously. However, this same system can prove to be harmful to our practice development if utilized as a form of micromanagement or as a substitute for leadership.

There is a common misconception that by monitoring our systems we are somehow fulfilling our leadership responsibilities, when, in fact, leadership has nothing in common with systems management. Routinely, we waste our time by failing to delegate the task of monitoring our systems, or if we do choose to delegate this task, we tend to micromanage the process and frustrate our staff by creating rigidity which is inherent in most systems and amplified by micromanagement. Rigid systems stifle creativity and spontaneity, the critical precursor to teamwork and our staff's sense of self worth as vital, contributing team members.

The reason that we gravitate toward management rather than leadership is that managing is easier than leading. As Marcus Buckingham has stated, leadership involves serious introspection along with creativity and a future orientation. Management, on the other hand, is more reactive than creative and tends to be systems based.

The most detrimental aspect of systems management is that it allows us to function at a low but acceptable level of proficiency, and without the knowledge that better systems (i.e., values-based leadership) exist, we are forced to accept the status quo. Jim Collins states that good is the enemy of great, and systems management is a perfect example of this concept.

As I stated at the beginning of the book, it is my belief that good practices can be managed, but great practices must be led. Implicit in this belief is the assumption that in order to create a great practice we must possess the knowledge, confidence, and competency to lead. Unfortunately, this is not always the case, and because we lack these vital resources, we cannot visualize the potential that true values-based leadership can provide for our practices. As a result, we accept mediocrity because without the knowledge and vision of a greater potential there is no compulsion to change.

TAKE-HOME MESSAGES FROM CHAPTER FIVE

- The leadership paradox relates to the fact that in spite of our extensive education as health care providers, we have no business education or training in areas that, according to noted business authorities, are key factors to our success as entrepreneurs.

- Leadership is the key success factor in transforming a practice from good to great.

- Systems management is a poor substitute for leadership.

- Systems management allows us to function at a low, but adequate, level of proficiency, and often hinders our motivation for improvement.

- Good practices can be managed, but great practices must be led.

Chapter 6

Managing Process

"Successful leaders spend a lot of time creating the identity of the organization—what our values are, what our mission is, what our purpose is, how we are going to act together as one. Those are agreements of how we are going to be together. You can actually get a whole team or a whole group to hold one another accountable. The team self-regulates and members call each other in a much more immediate way than a leader can ever do."

Margaret Wheatley—Founder and president emerita of the Berkana Institute, a global charitable foundation.

Their choice:

One of the greatest benefits of a mature, well-defined practice culture is that it allows us to move beyond the management of people to the management of process. No longer do we have to deal with issues like absenteeism, bad attitude, or lack of motivation on the part of our staff. These and other self-defeating, energy-draining personality traits do not exist in a mature culture. Quite simply, they are not tolerated.

I believe that joining a committed team that is guided by a well-defined culture is a conscious choice that must be made by each willing participant. If we have been diligent leaders, we will have intentionally created a culture that is so well-defined that the choice will be crystal clear. Our organization's culture should send a bold message to those who would join us that "This is who we are, and this is what we stand for. Love us or leave us!" Adopting the prevailing culture becomes the price of admission for each participant. Having said this, adopting the culture is only the first step to becoming a contributing member. Engaging in the culture is what keeps them in the game.

Small businesses such as health-care practices offer no hiding place for aberrant behavior. There is no place for someone who philosophically adopts the underlying principles of the culture but chooses to only partially engage in the work at hand. This type of behavior may be possible in a large corporation with large numbers of employees and a hierarchical leadership and management, but in a small enterprise where we exist in a face-to-face relationship, one's willingness to engage in the work of promoting the practice and its culture is front and center.

If we have taken Jim Collins's advice and placed the right people on the bus, and if we have provided them with a well-defined core ideology as a perpetual reference point and given them adequate training and resources to be successful, we will have created the environment necessary for the development of a committed team that is fully engaged in the perpetuation of the practice and its culture. Marcus Buckingham suggests that a team of highly committed professionals need only know the desired end result. They will find the best possible path to achieving the result. There is no need to manage the people. We simply need to observe and manage the process. Understanding that becoming and remaining part of our team is a conscious choice that must be made by each team member frees us as team leaders from the incorrect assumption that we are somehow responsible for molding individual behavior. Nothing could be further from the truth. We cannot mold people. We can, however, provide them with a clear vision of what is required to become and remain a member of our team.

Several years ago I had a dental assistant who was struggling emotionally. She had a rough upbringing in a small town in Louisiana. Her parents had died while she was still quite young, and she was raised by her older sister. She was divorced and estranged from her son and daughter-in-law who lived in Louisiana, but she dearly loved her grandchildren even though she seldom saw them. Darla was quiet by nature. She was a hard worker and very loyal to me and the practice. Unfortunately, her entire demeanor changed dramatically after her sister was diagnosed with cancer and died shortly thereafter. Darla withdrew within herself. She became moody and distant. It was obvious that she was grieving internally.

Darla's internal struggle was affecting the quality of her care as well as her relationship with other team members. It became obvious to all of us that Darla had become disengaged. Out of concern for her, I made a personal commitment to do all that I could do to help her regain her life and her position as a fully engaged and committed team member. I provided her with professional counseling, but after one or two sessions, she failed to return for her therapy. Nothing I did or said seemed to help resolve the situation, and with each passing day her relationship with our team and the quality of her care diminished.

Finally, I accepted the fact that I needed to terminate Darla for the benefit of the team and our culture. I decided however to try one last time to help Darla realize that she was about to lose her job. Debbie, our office manager, and I met with Darla the next day after work. At that meeting, I reaffirmed our desire to have her remain in our practice as a fully engaged participant. I told her that the decision to stay or leave was not mine, but hers. She had to make a choice to recommit to the principles and values that were at the core of our culture or she needed to leave. There was no need to revisit these principles and values. She, like every team member, knew what our culture demanded of her.

Darla sat quietly, with tears in her eyes, and listened to all that I had to say. She asked to have some time to consider my proposal. This was the end of our conversation.

The next day, before our morning staff meeting, Darla came to visit me. She entered my office and burst into tears. My first assumption was that these were tears of remorse. I was wrong. Darla told me that after our previous conversation she began to consider her options. It was then that she suddenly experienced an incredible epiphany. She realized, with absolute clarity, that her suffering was a manifestation of her extreme loneliness. She also realized how much she wanted to return to Louisiana to repair her relationship with her son and daughter-in-law and to spend time with her grandchildren. She gave me a hug, asked for my forgiveness, thanked me for all of my help, and resigned her position. Within a month she had moved back to Louisiana. To this day, I have never felt so good about letting someone go.

I share this story because I want to make it clear that once we have done our due diligence by creating a well-defined culture, we no longer have to be burdened by managing people. We are now free to move on to the more efficient and infinitely more productive realm of managing process. Having people who want to be team members because they believe in the culture and choose to engage in it creates a self-motivating environment that demands high standards from its members. Those who choose not to adhere to these standards will not last long in this environment.

Having created a self-managing team enables us to direct our full energy to managing process; an area that requires our creativity. Because we can manage process and define the essential ingredients of our practices' success, we are able to creatively adapt our efforts to meet goals that complement our overall strategy. To accomplish this, we must narrow our focus and concentrate maximum energy and effort on those areas we have identified as our keys to success. This application of creative thinking is what distinguishes us and our practices from the competition.

Our promise:

"Leaders who exhibit adequate amounts of self-confidence are more likely driven to empower their followers and share power. These leaders make sure that empowered followers have the knowledge, skills, and resources to accomplish the tasks for which they are responsible. To an outside observer, it may appear as though the leader is giving up control. In reality, the leader has first taken action to ensure that followers will succeed. In contrast, leaders who cannot share power and empower others, who cannot trust others with a degree of control (micromanagers), actually feel that they cannot trust themselves. What they have lost is their own self-control. This almost always guarantees their failure."

Molly and Marshall Sashkin—*Leadership That Matters*

Imagine, if you will, what life would be like if nothing that you did mattered. How would you feel if your words or your actions were so inconsequential that you were disregarded by others, and you became powerless and unable to alter your existence? Now consider what we do when we micromanage our staff. Is there really any difference between micromanaging people and making them inconsequential? If we deny them the ability to contribute and utilize their minds and their creativity have we not made them insignificant?

Without confidence that their actions matter, our staff will develop paralysis that is manifested by an absence of spontaneity and creativity in our practice culture. B. F. Skinner, a social psychologist, in a classic experiment, demonstrated that rats that were conditioned to believe that their actions were useless in altering their environment exhibited paralysis and failed to act when placed in a life-threatening situation. Conversely, rats that were conditioned to believe that their actions made a difference would act defensively when placed in a similar situation.

Micromanagement is the result of leadership by default. It is a means of compensating for our deficiencies as leaders. Disengaged leaders are like plumbers who fix leaks with duct tape because they have no tools. Micromanagement has become our leadership duct tape. We use it because we have no other tools in our bag.

Default leadership is arguably the greatest limiting factor for transforming our practices from good to great. For many of us, micromanagement is actually default leadership in disguise. We mistakenly believe that by overseeing and directing our staff and everything they do we are actually leading, when in reality we are unwittingly destroying our ability to provide effective leadership. This is because a professional practice that is micromanaged is by necessity burdened with excessive rules and regulations that demand compliance, and a compliant culture suppresses creativity and participative decision making.

Numerous studies have investigated the effect of micromanaged cultures versus participative cultures on a corporation's bottom line. John Zenger, in his book *The Extraordinary Leader*, cites a study which found that CEOs who stressed effective communication, accountability, and the empowerment of people were able to provide a much higher profit margin for their companies than their counterparts who emphasized performance monitoring. A research study conducted by Success Profiles found that companies who encouraged participative decision making had an overall 11.1 percent rate of compounded revenue growth compared to an overall 2.3 percent growth rate for those companies who did not encourage participation by their employees.

Another provocative study, cited in Daniel Goleman's book *Primal Leadership*, offers convincing evidence that our staff is the best and most accurate source for assessing us as leaders. In this longitudinal study of the effectiveness of leaders, the staff's assessment of the leader proved to be the most accurate in predicting the leader's success and effectiveness when compared to the assessment of the leader's peers and bosses. Even at seven years following the assessment, the staff's prediction of the leader's success was shown to be the most accurate. In the final analysis, the accuracy of the staff's prediction of the leader's success was equal if not superior to an elaborate battery of performance simulations performed in assessment centers.

What a profound irony! The very people that we unknowingly make insignificant by diminishing their role in our practice are the ones that possess the insight to make us better leaders. Considering this revelation, perhaps we should begin to listen to what they have to say, or better yet, we might consider adopting a 360-degree performance evaluation that includes their assessment of our performance.

So what's to be learned from all of this information? First, we must promise ourselves and our staff that we will honor and respect their choice to adopt our culture and participate in our practice. This is best done by making them relevant—by becoming passionate advocates of a participative culture.

Second, we must promise ourselves that we will no longer lead by default. The argument for purposeful leadership is too strong and the consequences of default leadership are too significant. We must quit wasting our time and precious energy on trivial matters and instead concentrate our efforts on matters of greater importance to our practices and our professions. And last, it is time for us to seek partnerships with institutions of higher learning so that we can focus our energy on teaching industry-specific leadership qualities that will enable us to eradicate leadership deficiencies in the health-care community.

TAKE-HOME MESSAGES FROM CHAPTER SIX

- Successful leaders create cultures that allow them to move beyond the lower-level function of people management to the higher-level function of process management.

- We cannot mold people, therefore our organization's culture should be so well-defined that potential team members can easily decide if they want to join and engage. It is their choice.

- Micromanagement reduces a person's relevance and diminishes their willingness to contribute and engage in our organization.

- Default leadership is arguably the greatest limiting factor for transforming our practices from good to great.

- We micromanage because that is all we know to do.

- Our staff has the information we need to be better leaders. We should consider adopting 360-degree evaluations for our practices so we can acquire this vital information.

- We should become passionate advocates of a participative culture.

Chapter 7

The Culture Is the Brand

"A company's external customer service is only as strong as the company's internal leadership, and the culture of commitment that this leadership creates. If the service messages are out of step with what's ultimately experienced by customers, marketing dollars are wasted. And customer dissatisfaction rises right along with staff turnover."

Jim Clemmer—*The Leader's Digest*

"A brand by definition is an identifiable product, service, person, or place, augmented in such a way that the buyer or user perceives relevant, unique, sustainable added values which match their needs most closely. Depending on the market, up to 70% of the earnings can be attributed to the brand."

Jan Lindemann

Branding has become a hot topic in the world of business. An online search of Amazon.com indicates that there are over 2,500 books available on the topic of branding. Another search of the Harvard Business Review online found over 900 scholarly papers have been written for this publication on the topic of branding. Of these 900 papers, a significant majority were written within the past ten years.

What is a brand and why is it so important? How is branding different for a small service-oriented business versus a large corporate manufacturer? Does size matter when it comes to a brand? Finally, and most importantly, what constitutes a brand for a health-care enterprise, and what does it do for our practices? These are some of the questions that we must answer before developing a brand strategy for our practices.

First, we should begin with a discussion of what branding is not. One of the most commonly held misconceptions is that branding is all about advertising. Although advertising is a tool that is often used to achieve effective branding, it is only part of the equation. A brand is, in fact, much more than a tag line and a logo. An icon or symbol, like a logo, represents a product or service by recreating emotions evoked by the customer's experience of the product or service. At the heart of the brand are the product or service's deeper, intrinsic factors which, although intangible, create the emotional response that attracts the customer.

There are both tangible and intangible components of a brand. The tangible components include a business's core competencies, marketing, and the actual product that they provide. The intangibles, which are equally if not more important to the brand, are emotional and derived from the client's experience of the business and its product. These gut-level emotions are essential prerequisites of successful branding, as stated by Leslie de Chernatony: "In today's environment, a brand's sustainable competitive advantage is based not so much on what customers receive [tangible], but rather on how customers receive it [intangible]."

Further validation of this hypothesis comes from various business scholars who claim that the modern consumer is suffering from information overload and, out of necessity, has developed a form of cognitive immunity to unsolicited information in the form of advertising. Consequently, advertising is becoming less effective as a means of delivering our brand's message, whereas the emotional (intangible) aspects of our brand are becoming increasingly significant.

Another misconception is that marketing creates the brand, when in fact the opposite is true. Consider the last time you responded to a business's advertisement only to be disappointed when the company was unable to fulfill the advertisement's promises. If you are like me, you were so disappointed that the company broke their promise that you would never again consider doing business with them. The point is that a brand is a promise. It is a promise made between us and our customers, and, as such, we must be sure that we can deliver on our promise before we make it. This requires that we first create a brand vision based on our core competencies, and then implement systems that insure that we can deliver the brand promise consistently to our customers. Essential to delivering the brand promise is a staff that believes in the brand and is capable of fulfilling the brand promise. Once all of these ingredients are in place, a brand strategy is implemented. This would include marketing that makes the brand promise based on our known capabilities to consistently deliver on the promise.

The goal of branding is to create brand loyalty, whereby customers will choose to purchase or reuse the product or service in the future. The strength of the brand loyalty is indicated by the degree to which the customer will remain loyal to a given product or service even when competing brands are more readily available or more competitively priced. The brand promise in the form of advertising may be what gets the customers in the door, but it is our ability to deliver on the promise that creates brand loyalty and keeps them coming back and referring their friends and family. In this respect, there are significant differences between a large manufacturer and a small service-oriented business with regard to branding.

In a corporate environment, especially in large corporations, the corporate culture and product brand are quite distinguishable from the perspective of the end user. For example, you might prefer to purchase a certain brand of running shoe even though this shoe is more difficult to find and more expensive than other similar brands. Brand loyalty to a shoe, however, says nothing about the culture of the company that produced the shoe. The shoe may have been manufactured by child labor in an overseas sweatshop. The consumer may be unaware of these dysfunctional aspects of the company. They may never see the manufacturing facility or experience the culture of the organization. They simply like the shoe.

In a microenterprise like a health-care practice, or in any small business in the service industry, there is direct contact with the end user of the service. The patient personally experiences the culture of the business. There are no distributors and vendors to intervene. The patient purchases a service which is provided by a person who directly represents the organization and its culture. Whether it is the health-care provider or a staff member, this person is, in the eyes of the patient, the visual manifestation of the practice's brand and culture. In this context, the organization's brand and culture are indistinguishable to the patient. The ultimate goal of any service-oriented business is to develop a brand promise based on the company's core competencies, and to develop their culture, staff, and supporting systems that enable them to consistently deliver on the promise so that they can reach a critical mass of brand-loyal customers. This then becomes the tipping point at which more new customers are gained through word-of-mouth referrals than through advertising. It is at this point that the business experiences exponential rather than linear growth.

It is important to remember when considering our practice brand that, as a small service-oriented business, the health-care practitioner creates the culture, and the culture drives the brand. More importantly, however, it is the staff that drives the culture. So if we want a strong brand that promotes brand loyalty, i.e., repeat business, we need to invest our time and resources in developing the people in our business. This begins by finding the right people, who share our core ideology and believe in our brand. Then we must provide them with the training, resources, and support to be successful.

I recently conducted an analysis of touch points in my practice. A touch point is an interaction with a potential customer. It includes actual face-to-face interactions with customers, such as speaking to them when they call for information or an appointment, or greeting them when they walk through the door.

Touch points also include high-tech interactions, such as automated phone systems and websites. Advertisements in the form of print ads and mailers are also considered to be touch points.

Touch Points (NTEA)

STAFF		DOCTORS	
Function	Time (min)	Function	Time (min)
Scheduling	10	MH review	10
Greeting	5	Examination	10
Diagnosis & MH	20	Treatment	60
Treatment	80	PO review	5
PO instructions	5	Recall	5
Check out	10		
PO call	5		
Recall	15		
TOTAL	150	TOTAL	90

This is a worthwhile exercise and one that I would recommend for a staff meeting. Just list all of the encounters that patients have with people in your practice. Then separate the list into patient encounters with the doctor versus patient encounters with the staff. If you are like me, you will be amazed at the total number of touch points you and your staff can identify. Even more amazing is the fact that the patients encounter your staff far more frequently than they do you. There are important lessons to be learned from this exercise. One lesson worth learning is that if we, as our practice's leader, expect loyal patients, we had better create a culture that nurtures brand loyalty. Even though it is the staff that drives the culture, it is the leader that creates the culture. If we accept the premise that culture is the shadow of the leader, then we have to take either the credit or the blame for the organization's culture. There is no excuse for a poor culture. If we are responsible for defining the core ideology which serves as the anchor for our culture, for clearly communicating our culture's objectives based on this core ideology, and for hiring people that are aligned with these objectives and values, then we own the culture. Having a poor culture and being unable to fulfill our brand promise means that we have failed as leaders.

Building your brand starts from within. Even though it's eventually about the external view of your business, the one and only true way to build your brand is from the inside out. William Taylor, the cofounder of *Fast Company* magazine, states that "You can't be special, distinctive, and compelling in the marketplace unless you create something special, distinctive, and compelling in the workplace."

TAKE-HOME MESSAGES FROM CHAPTER SEVEN

- Modern consumers are suffering from information overload in the form of advertisements. Brand strength is becoming less affected by advertising and marketing, and more a function of our patients' intangible emotional experience of our organization.

- A brand is a promise that an organization makes to its clients. Fulfilling the promise is what keeps them as clients.

- As the size of the organization decreases to a microenterprise, the culture and the brand become indistinguishable.

- Leaders create a culture, but it is the staff that drives the culture and ultimately the brand of a microenterprise.

- Brands must be built from the inside out.

Chapter 8

The Legacy

"I am convinced that it is not the fear of death, of our lives ending, that haunts our sleep so much as the fear ... that as far as the world is concerned, we might never have lived."

Harold Kushner

A significant part of what I do as a transition specialist is help doctors prepare their practices for sale. This process begins several years before the anticipated sale. "Exit Planning," as it is called, is a multifaceted process that involves the coordination of attorneys, CPAs, financial planners, insurance specialists, and practice brokers. All of this coordinated effort is intended to serve one purpose—to design and implement a process that allows the doctor to exit clinical practice according to a predetermined plan.

Being a clinical dentist for many years has allowed me to view this process from a unique perspective. I understand that leaving practice is one thing, but what you leave behind is another story entirely.

While developing the exit planning program for Phase Two Associates, I decided early on that I wanted to do more than create an "escape route" for worn-out, disillusioned doctors. I've always felt that exit planning should have as much to do with the person as it does with the practice. I want to see doctors finish their professional careers like a marathoner who finishes strong, and I want them to appreciate the long journey as much as the well-deserved victory.

There is an old adage which states that there are few certainties in life other than death and taxes. I would add to that the certainty that we will someday exit our clinical practices. How we exit our practices may not be of our choosing. Death or disabilities unfortunately have a way of short-circuiting the best of plans. But what we leave behind is fully within our control.

I read an article recently that suggested that as we age we develop a psychological need to move from the realm of success to significance. I have a difficult time accepting the premise that the need for significance is somehow related to age. I know from my own personal experiences with young professionals that they greatly value and seek significance in their personal and professional lives. I have made a point of discussing the importance of significance with our young dentists whenever I have an opportunity to speak at their schools or meetings. I want them to understand that success and significance are not mutually exclusive. In fact, I question whether there can be true success without significance. I believe that they are one and the same for those of us that seek deeper meaning in our lives.

If we leave our profession and leave nothing behind for our successors but a few dental chairs and an office, we have cheated both ourselves and our profession. Our legacy should be much more than a few tangible items. When someone asks my successors what I left behind, I hope they have more to show than a broken down dental chair sitting in an unused operatory. I hope they can say that I left them a legacy of leadership and fulfillment that has served them well throughout their careers. Most importantly, I want them to say that I left them their most valued possession—a roadmap to significance.

My life has been impacted by the legacy I received from a mentor leader. If it were not for Dr. Frank Trice, I would most assuredly not be where I am today. As a young dental student I came to know Frank through my role as class president and his role as the dean of students at the University of Texas Dental Branch in Houston.

Frank was an endodontist who rose through the ranks to become president of our national association. He was a tall, lanky, east Texan, whose slow, deliberate speech and awkward appearance belied the fact that he was a true mentor leader. Without question, Frank was as authentic as they come.

It has been said that certain people have a unique brain function that allows them to mentally connect with other people. Frank was one of those people, or at least he was as far as I was concerned. When we spoke there were no pretenses or hidden agendas.

I learned from him what it meant to lead for the benefit of others. Frank was always there for me as well as for any student at the dental branch. I will always remember Frank telling me about the secret dean's fund that was created to give interest-free loans to students that were in need of financial assistance. Frank asked me to spread the word to my fellow students that the fund was available. No notes were signed, and the debt could be repaid whenever the funds were available.

One day while talking with Dr. Olsen, the dean of the dental school, I thanked him for providing this service for us. Dr. Olsen laughed and informed me that there was no such fund. The money came directly from Frank.

Frank saw in me capabilities and qualities that I never knew I possessed. He believed in me and stood beside me during difficult times in my life, and when it came time for me to apply to the endodontic residency program he made sure that I was given every possible consideration. He taught me what it meant to be a "mentor leader" and the importance of giving back to our profession. I can only hope that each of us will someday do for a young health-care practitioner what Frank did for me.

Each of us has the ability to create a legacy of significance, but to leave something behind, we must first possess it. Leadership is a perfect vehicle for achieving significance because it is, by its very nature, other-focused. Leadership is not a position, but rather an emotional connection between a leader and a follower. No one can lead without this emotional connection, and we connect by making leadership about them, not us.

The more we focus our attention and direct our efforts outwardly, the stronger the connection we create with our followers, and the more we become what Tony Dungy describes as a mentor leader. Such leadership is characterized by our willingness as leaders to abandon our lecturing and to come down from our soapbox so that we can walk beside those we lead. This form of face-to-face leadership can only be effective if we lower our shields and accept the vulnerability that makes us human. By becoming more authentic, we become more human, and we elevate ourselves and our message to a level of significance that removes all of the barriers that stand between us and those we lead.

What a wonderful and enduring gift it would be to leave a young professional the roadmap to significance through leadership. Think of what it would mean if each of us could learn to lead for the benefit of others and then pass this knowledge and commitment on to our successors. Think of how much more fulfilled they would be having acquired this skill and knowledge early in their professional careers rather than desperately seeking validation for their years of clinical practice as they near retirement. I find the contrast between these two scenarios to be quite striking and sobering.

Consider also what a legacy of leadership would mean to the future of our professions. Developing a core of young mentor leaders who are committed to perpetuating this legacy will, over time, create an exponential growth of effective leadership within our health-care professions. I can think of no greater need for the health-care profession, at this critical point in history, than an increase of leaders from within our ranks. It will be these leaders that someday take back the reins of health-care reform and dictate its future course based on the needs of our patients.

Throughout my life I have always held the belief that good begets good, or as some might say, what goes around comes around. There is no greater example of the underlying truth to this statement than our commitment to leave a legacy of leadership.

TAKE-HOME MESSAGES FROM CHAPTER EIGHT

- Exiting our practices is a certainty. How we exit our practices is a matter of choice.

- Significance is important to young and old alike.

- In order to leave something as a legacy, we must first possess it. A legacy of leadership is no different.

- We connect with others by making leadership about them, not us.

- As we become more authentic, we become more human, and our message is heard clearly because there are no longer barriers that stand between us and those we lead.

If you're a fan of this book, please tell others…

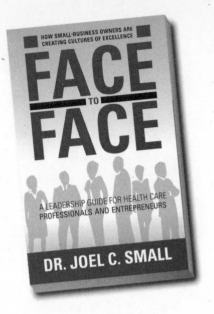

- Write about *Face To Face* on your blog, Twitter, MySpace, and Facebook page.

- Suggest *Face To Face* to friends.

- When you're in a bookstore, ask them if they carry the book. The book is available through all major distributors, so any bookstore that does not have *Face To Face* in stock can easily order it.

- Write a positive review of *Face To Face* on www.amazon.com.

- Send my publisher, HigherLife Publishing, suggestions on Web sites, conferences, and events you know of where this book could be offered at media@ahigherlife.com.

- Purchase additional copies to give away as gifts.

Connect with me…

To learn more about Face To Face, please email me at jsmalldds@phasetwoassociates.com or visit www.readfacetoface.com.

You may also contact my publisher directly:

HigherLife Publishing

400 Fontana Circle

Building 1 – Suite 105

Oviedo, Florida 32765

Phone: (407) 563-4806

Email: media@ahigherlife.com